WILDERNESS
AS METAPHOR FOR GOD
IN THE HEBREW BIBLE

Robert Miller's new book provides a rich and nuanced account of the desert. He transforms it from an abstract metaphor into a place that is real, strange, precarious and tenacious.
Dr. Nathan MacDonald, Reader in the Interpretation of the Old Testament, Cambridge University

Robert Miller's *Wilderness as Metaphor for God in the Hebrew Bible* is a concise but rich Biblical-spiritual deconstruction of the "South". "Going south" in common vernacular either denotes an unfortunate turn of events or it is uncritically romanticised. Miller successfully indicates the paradoxical nature of the "South" – the desert – as both a place and a presence in which paradox is the guiding hermeneutical principle and he rightly relates it to a paradoxical God who is both hidden and revealed and experienced as both desolate and abundant. This is in line with the very nature of a metaphor, which has an "is" and an "is not" dual character. As such, Miller's work makes a valuable contribution to Christian spirituality in general and mystic Christian spirituality in particular. It connects multiple disciplines and therefore theologians and students interested in Christian spirituality and the formation of God-images and God-language will find Miller's work particularly useful.
Dr Tanya van Wyk (Christian spirituality and Christian ethics; Faculty of Theology and Religion, University of Pretoria, South Africa)

WILDERNESS
AS METAPHOR FOR GOD IN THE HEBREW BIBLE

ROBERT D. MILLER II, O.F.S.

sussex
ACADEMIC
PRESS
Brighton • Chicago • Toronto

Copyright © Robert D. Miller II, 2022.

The right of Robert D. Miller II to be identified as Author of this work has been asserted in accordance with the Copyright, Designs and Patents Act 1988.

2 4 6 8 10 9 7 5 3 1

Nihil Obstat:
Rev. Christopher Begg, S.T.D., Ph.D.
Censor Deputatis

Imprimatur:
Very Reverend Daniel B. Carson
Vicar General and Moderator of the Curia
Archdiocese of Washington
June 16, 2021

The *nihil obstat* and *imprimatur* are official declarations that a book or pamphlet is free of doctrinal or moral error. There is no implication that those who have granted the *nihil obstat* and the *imprimatur* agree with the content, opinions or statements expressed therein.

First published in Great Britain in 2022 by
SUSSEX ACADEMIC PRESS
PO Box 139, Eastbourne BN24 9BP

Distributed in North America by
SUSSEX ACADEMIC PRESS
Independent Publishers Group
814 N. Franklin Street
Chicago, IL 60610

All rights reserved. Except for the quotation of short passages for the purposes of criticism and review, no part of this publication may be reproduced, stored in a retrieval system, or transmitted, in any form or by any means, electronic, mechanical, photocopying, recording or otherwise, without the prior permission of the publisher.

British Library Cataloguing in Publication Data
A CIP catalogue record for this book is available from the British Library.

Library of Congress Cataloging-in-Publication Data
To be applied For.

Paperback ISBN 978-1-78976-107-8

Typeset and designed by Sussex Academic Press, Brighton & Eastbourne.

CONTENTS

Preface   vii

I
Introduction   1

II
Yahweh from the South   5

III
The Corporal Desert   10

IV
Participant Observation   16

V
Desert Wind   22

VI
The Textual Desert   25

VII
The Folkloric Desert   34

Contents

VIII
Caveats   46

IX
Conclusion   49

Notes   53
Bibliography   84
Index   102

PREFACE

This short study emerged as an addendum. In *Yahweh: Origins of the Desert God* (Forschungen zur Religion und Literatur des Alten und Neuen Testaments 284; Göttingen: Vandenhoeck & Ruprecht, 2021), I explored biblical associations of a God named Yahweh with regions to the south of Israel and Judah in connection with Ancient Near Eastern texts and archaeology to build a historical model for the introduction of Yahwism from Midian to Israel. One might easily argue, however, that such a study ignores the most important aspect of the biblical texts it examined: their meaning. The present monograph addresses some of these same texts in hopes of *interpretation*, rather than historical reconstruction.

My interpretation is theological, not in the sense that it has something to contribute to contemporary theological discourse—although perhaps it does.[1] It is theological in its focus on a theological notion encapsulated by associating God with "The South." Since that notion is literally "about God," it is theo-logical. The goal of this exposition of the biblical text is to emphasize what each passage meant to the ancient Israelite audience with a view to what it means to the modern reader. I approach the Hebrew Bible as a literary work. This means that the primary focus is not so much on the world behind the text or the components from which the text was produced (although these are not irrelevant or ignored) as on the world *created by* the text in its engagement with ancient readers of its final form. That world-creation is both *historical*, in that it depends on the

Preface

historical setting of the ancient readers, and *literary*, in that it operates through the synchronic elements of the text.

And yet, this is a work of Biblical Theology; one might even say Biblical Spirituality. I endeavor to assist the reader enter more fully into the richness of the theology found in the Hebrew Bible, but not by a "paraenetic" presentation of the text's enduring relevance to today's theological issues. Rather, I help the reader hear anew the text's own theological vision.

Perhaps it is best to consider this study, then, a hermeneutical exploration of one aspect of the text, hermeneutical in the sense of mediating between culture and philosophy, both ancient and contemporary.[2] Hermeneutics is "the knowledge and technical norms which permit one to read, relate, and interpret relations and meanings in a given culture."[3] Theophilus Okere calls hermeneutics the "study of that great and most human characteristic which is the effort to give meaning to life."[4] The biblical authors—and many biblical readers—give meaning to life in their depiction and rendition of God,[5] and as this study will show, the desert archetype provides a mythic cypher for the divine that ordinary discourse could not express. Our task will be to unpack the symbolizing processes biblical authors used, drawing on cognitive science, intertextuality, and ethnographic analogy, to recover the ontological reality behind the archetype.[6]

There are numerous individuals and organizations that I owe many thanks to for their help in this enterprise. The School of Theology and Religious Studies at The Catholic University of America granted me a sabbatical where most of the research took place. I thank the Master and Fellows of St. John's College, Cambridge, for naming me a Beaufort Overseas Visiting Scholar to pursue that research, at the invitation of Dr. Nathan MacDonald. Questions, discussion, and suggestions of Jean Szlamowicz, Christian Sahner, Carol Barrett-Ford, Rosalie Maloney, and others on this particular

Preface

aspect of the larger Yahweh project were indispensable. My research assistants, Howard Jung and Joshua Roye, provided extensive, thorough editing, for which I am most grateful.

I
Introduction

Introduction

"THE LORD CAME WITH MYRIADS OF HOLY ONES from the south, from his mountain slopes" (Deut 33,2). A poetic snippet, among the earliest in the Hebrew Bible, reappears in similar form in biblical passages from the 11th to the 5th centuries BC: Judg 5,4–5; Hab 3,3; Ps 68,8–9; and Zech 9,14. From an early period, biblical authors perceived the South— the desert region variously named Teman, Seir, Paran—as God's domain. "God came from Teman", says Hab 3,3. And this is not about the Exodus; this metaphor of God's procession from a southern desert region is not about the Exodus of *Israelites* via Sinai, for it is here *God* who "went forth from Seir" (Judg 5,4). Rather, the image is a "horizontal theophany": God "shone forth from Mount Paran" (Deut 33,2), usually assigned to a mythic antiquity—"When you marched from the desert" (Ps 68,8)—but in other texts suspended until the end of time, as in Zech 9,14: "He will come in the storms of the South".

For a century, scholars have rightly suggested this association has to do with historical *origins* of a deity named Yahweh in those southern regions.[1] Yet scholarly analysis of these phrases has neglected the actual literary and theological function of these texts and of this image.[2] In other words, while these texts may tell us something about the origins of Yahw*ism*, they are also a statement about Yahweh.[3] The metaphorical theophany of God "from the South" presupposes and encapsulates mythological ideas. By making the South God's domain, the biblical tradition says something about Yahweh and his character.[4]

What is more, the biblical association of God with the South repeatedly includes place-names Edom and Midian in the face of the overwhelming animus against Edom and Midian (for Edom, Num 20,14–20; 2 Sam 9,14–22; 2 Kgs 8,20–22; 2 Chron 20,10–23; Ps 60,8; 108,9; 137,7; Obad 1,11–14; Isa 34,5–8; and Jer 49,7–22; for Midian, Gen 37,28; Num 25,6–15; 31,1.17; Judg 6,1–9). Although that

Introduction

persistence may be partially due to a historical reality of the origins of Yahwism, it is certainly also because of a theological claim that biblical authors thought they could not do without.

This study elucidates that claim, explaining what it means that Yahweh is "of the South". The traditions of the God of the South—regardless of their origin—are an important part of the biblical mythos, and for all the diachronic development in the history of Israel, they can be elucidated as a piece.

Landscape-based traditions are mythic imaginations that have "geographical boundaries like islands, continents, and countries".[5] As Carole Crumley writes, because meanings attributed to nature "give societies their character and inform their actions, a critical narrative of human-environment relationships can also be read in the landscape".[6] Such landscape traditions last a long time in a particular area. Certainly, they are adapted, but they change considerably less than legends do.[7] This is true even when the landscape itself changes.[8]

Two initial caveats must be made. First, the Hebrew Bible sets up no "desert ideal" as the quintessence of biblical religion, a favorite nostrum of eighteenth and nineteenth century scholarship.[9] The Bible does not present desert life as an ideal, and no reform movements in ancient Israel advocated a return to nomadic spirituality.[10]

Second, it should be noted that we can conflate "the South" of most of our biblical passages with "the desert" of Ps 68,8. For an Israelite living in Israel or Judah, the South would be a homogenous image, bringing to mind not the Gulf of Aqaba but the mountainous desert of what is today called the Negev, the Aravah, Jordan's Wadi Rum, Arabia's Hejaz, and the Sinai Peninsula—what the World Wildlife Fund calls the "Arabian Desert and East Saharo-Arabian xeric shrublands".[11] The constancy of the correlation of "South" with

Introduction

"desert" is one factor that contributes to the stability of the associated traditions.[12]

As Jean Szlamowicz writes, "Vocabulary may denote things that we view as objects existing in the world, but language only ever designates within a given context of communicative intention".[13] To find the cultural value of the linguistic sign of the South or desert, we must unpack what the mythic South, the desert, meant to ancient Israelites, the desert landscape's significance as a symbolic resource to the biblical authors.[14] Use of terms like "symbolic resource", "imagery", and "archetype" is not meant to be nebulous. The world of perception, especially of the natural world, is open to being treated symbolically, and such symbolism is concomitant with religion.[15] "The wilderness" is imagined as a place; it becomes a landscape,[16] and thus is much more than a metaphor.[17] To understand this imaginative process requires "a continuous dialectical tacking between the most local of local detail and the most global of global structure in such a way as to bring both into view simultaneously".[18] As Clifford Geertz laid out for his own ethnographic work, what follows will oscillate "restlessly between the sort of exotic minutiae (lexical antitheses, categorical schemes, morphophonemic transformations) that make even the best ethnographies a trial to read and the sort of sweeping characterizations ('quietism,' 'dramatism,' 'contextualism') that makes all but the most pedestrian of them implausible".[19]

II

YAHWEH FROM THE SOUTH

Yahweh from the South

WE BEGIN WITH A SET OF SUPPOSEDLY EARLY TEXTS that all say something about the origin of Yahweh in the south, although more that geography links them together.[1] These passages have been analyzed in a variety of ways, but we can think of them as folklore. Most of the Hebrew Bible emerged in an oral-and-written culture,[2] and such a society's literature should be studied just as modern folklore is.[3] What we have in this particular case are four or five closely related variants of Recurrent Multi-word Sequences (RMS).[4] They are not exact formulas, and the variation itself is proof of their folkloric nature.[5] That they are now only preserved in writing does not change that fact.[6] Here is each in turn in my own translation.

Deuteronomy 33:2 reads,

> He said, "Yahweh came from Sinai
>   And dawned on him from Seir.
> He shone forth from Mount Paran
>   And went from his massif sanctuary,
> From his southland mountain slopes for them"

This is a poem of five trilexic stichs. The stichs list five locations from which God has come: Sinai, Seir, Paran, "massif sanctuary," and the mountain slopes. These locations are in parallel, but not identical. Only in this variant is Sinai one of the places from which God comes.

Seir can be synonymous with Edom, as it is in Ezekiel 35. Gen 14:6 and Josh 15:1–4 consider Seir to be that portion of Edom that is west of the Arabah, and this is the general usage. Paran overlaps with Edom but abuts the Wilderness of Zin between Kadesh and Edom (1 Kgs 11:17–18).

The second variant is Judges 5:4–5, which we will not discuss on its own.

Yahweh from the South

4 Yahweh, when you went out from Seir,
 When you marched from the territory of Edom,
 The earth shook, and also the heavens, they dripped.
 The clouds dripped water,
5 The mountains trembled,
 Before Yahweh, the One of Sinai,
 Before Yahweh, the God of Israel.

In Habakkuk 3:3, we have:

God (Eloah) came from Teman,
 The Holy One from Mount Paran.

In this brief excerpt, two new terms for the South are introduced. Teman may, in fact, simply mean "south" (Exod 26:18, 35; 27:9; 36:23; Num 2:10; 10:6; Deut 3:27; Josh 12:3; 15:1; Isa 43:6; Ps 78:26; Peshitta Job 37:17). If Teman is read as a proper geographic name, it is used in different ways in the Hebrew Bible. Ezek 25:13 uses the expression "Teman to Dedan" as a merism for the whole of Edom, which suggests a Cisjordanian location consistent with Habakkuk 3. In Genesis and Ezekiel, it is a place in Edom, either Cisjordanian (Ezek 20:46) or Transjordanian (Gen 36:34). It appears to be synonymous with Edom elsewhere (Amos 1:11–12; Obad 8–9; Jer 49:7, 20).

Psalm 68:8–9 is our next variant:

God, when you went forth before your people,
 When you marched through the desert, (Selah)
The earth quaked, the heavens poured
 Before God, the One of Sinai,
 Before God, the God of Israel.

This variant is quite close to Judges 5, except the proper geographical names are absent.

Yahweh from the South

Finally, Zechariah 9:14 should be considered alongside these other passages:

> And Yahweh will appear over them,
> And his arrow will go out as lightning.
> The Lord Yahweh will sound the shofar,
> And he will come in the storms of Teman.

I prefer to leave the final word as Teman, with the Modern English Version alone of contemporary translations, but only to show the parallels with the other variants—the word may well mean simply "south." Unlike the other variants, this one lacks the earth or mountains shaking, and indeed the sense of terror of the others.

The basic RMS in these variants is [NAME FOR GOD] CAME [OR MARCHED] FROM [SOUTHERN LOCALE]. This RMS occurs in DEUTERONOMY 33, JUDGES 5, HABAKKUK 3, and ZECHARIAH 9, although there the tense is future. PSALM 68 lacks even these basic integers, having only the image GOD and the motif GOD MARCHES.

Indexing the variants, there are seven registers:

1. YAHWEH CAME FROM SEIR—found in DEUTERONOMY 33 and JUDGES 5
2. [GOD] CAME FROM TEMAN—found in HABAKKUK 3 with "Eloah" (and ZECHARIAH 9 with Yahweh and Adonai-Yahweh)
3. [GOD] CAME FROM PARAN—found in HABAKKUK 3 with "Eloah" and in DEUTERONOMY 33 with Yahweh
4. [GOD] CAME FROM SINAI—found in DEUTERONOMY 33 with Yahweh
5. [GOD] CAME FROM EDOM—found in JUDGES 5 with Yahweh
6. [GOD] CAME FROM THE DESERT—found in PSALM 68 with Elohim

Yahweh from the South

GOD MARCHED FROM THE SOUTH is the basic theme. This requires that God has at one time resided in the South, in order for him to be able to come from there. From the South, he has approached Israel; he is not marching past Israel or to some other location. It is, therefore, a horizontal theophany, as well as a statement about God's abode and mobility.

III

The Corporal Desert

The Corporal Desert

WE CAN BEGIN TO UNPACK THESE PASSAGES with cognitive science.[1] Cognitive science is the interdisciplinary study of the mind, where philosophy, psychology, linguistics, cybernetics, and neuroscience intersect.[2] When it bears upon literature, cognitive science understands meaning as "the stuff that mental processing is made of; it involves the basic relation between mental content and the experience of the world".[3]

Mental dispositions depend on bodies[4]. Somatic sensations and physiological responses are the resources for cognitive processes to filter through cultural symbolic meanings.[5] So we must consider ancient Israelite bodies that because of travel for trade or military service would have experienced deserts.[6]

The deserts of Israelite bodily experience are real deserts, with the Köppen Climate Classification of "Hot Desert Climates" (BWh).[7] Average annual rainfall near Kadesh Barnea is 87 mm.[8] Archaeological and geomorphological studies show that environmental conditions were similar to those of today.[9]

Although, in the end, we are working with deserts *in literature*, not actual deserts but literary deserts of the Hebrew Bible, what Sten Moslund calls "topopoetics . . . the power of palatial experiences in literature",[10] nevertheless, the literary still depends on the physical.[11] As Moslund elucidates, drawing on Heidegger (*Poetry, Language, Thought*), Deleuze, and Guattari (*Kafka; What is Philosophy*), and on case studies from Guyana and the Kalahari, actual places both dictate language and are in turn defined by language.[12] This is an important distinction: while constructivists have rightly insisted for many decades that language gives shape to our understanding of every space, that there is no unmediated place,[13] more recent theorists are realizing that specific elements of topography are agents in how their own social function and, in this case, sacrality, is perceived.[14] There is an irreducible tension between active agents and landscape.[15] Both place and language, thereafter, in turn, guide sensation.[16] In other words, language depends on the sensual, so the literary desert depends on the physical desert, the extra-literary experience of which the words call up.[17] But since language also defines the desert, we will return to the literary desert, as well.

Deserts are foreign to the everyday life of the biblical authors, who were not nomadic pastoralists.[18] To their rarified environment of Jerusalem scribal culture, or even to the prophetic voice on the street corner of Samaria,[19] the desert would have been "desolate and still and strange . . . ", "barren, howling" in Deuteronomy's words (32,10). The desert was the opposite of the biblical author's urban environment, what Baudrillard called "an ecstatic critique of culture".[20] From what was learned through trade and travel, compounded by imagination,[21] the desert was "unfamiliar and often grotesque in its forms and colors, inhabited by rare, furtive creatures of incredible hardiness and cunning . . . "[22]—the Bible's snakes and scorpions (Deut 8,15), owls (Ps 102,6), porcupines (Isa 34,11), hyenas (Isa 34,14), and wolves (Jer 5,6).[23]

Cognitive science implicates the individual, his or her body and senses, as Merleau-Ponty argued: "Experience is not arrayed before me as if I were God, it is lived by me from a certain point of view; I am not the spectator, I am involved".[24] Sociologists have undertaken studies of wilderness experience that provide experimental data for our discussion.[25] Studies have found cognitive engagement with wilderness involves focused attention on small, varied details in comparison to other places.[26] Observed wildlife often captures attention.[27]

Thus, the great owl of Lev 11,17; Deut 14,16; and Isa 34,11 is the Egyptian Eagle-owl (*Bubo ascalaphus*), which inhabits ruins and caves.[28] The *šaḥap* of Lev 11,16 and Deut 14,15 is probably not a cuckoo or a seagull but the long-eared owl (*Asio otus otus*).²⁹ In complete darkness, this "winged assassin of the night"³⁰ swoops down on hares and rodents, cartwheeling in its own line of flight as it drops on its prey and kills it by a bite to the back of the skull, before either swallowing it whole or eviscerating it and leaving the entrails uneaten.³¹ Israelites knew it to be a silent predator, its flight muffled by comb-like fringe on the leading edge of its outer primary wings and downy surface on the dorsal side of its remige wings.³² They also knew desert rodents had adapted enlarged, hollow, bony structures that enclose the middle and inner ear to enable them to hear the long-eared owl.³³

The *qôs* or little owl that Ps 102,6–7 puts in the desert is *Athene persica*.³⁴ It nests in cavities of the vertical cliffs,³⁵ but it will also take over the food-filled burrows gerbils have dug in the desert floor,³⁶ having already come across the inhabitants as they slept and immediately devoured them.³⁷ The little owl is, as biblical writers knew, a fierce hunter, catching prey that weighs as much as the owl does itself.³⁸

Isaiah's hyenas will eat carcasses of almost any medium or large mammal (and occasionally tortoises), including their own dead, their powerful jaws cracking the large bones.³⁹ A goat eaten by hyenas will be devoured in entirety, except for the hooves.⁴⁰ Palestinian folklore says that hyenas will spray lost humans with urine that will drug them so they can be dragged back to the dens to be devoured.⁴¹

Israelites might even have known the Negev grasshopper, *Tmethis pulchripennis*, which "mimics sand so perfectly that it is almost impossible to detect it when it is immobile".⁴²

Alongside the animals, biblical writers knew the desert was "sparingly colonized by weird mutants from the plant kingdom, most of them as spiny, thorny, stunted and twisted as they are tenacious".⁴³ The most common perennial plant in Paran is *Cornulaca monocantha*, a straggling, branched, woody shrub with squat bluish-green, scale-like leaves that grasp its greyish, wiry stems.[44] The umbrella thorn acacia (*Vachellia tortilis*), the most frequent species of the wadis and flood plains, combines paired straight and paired hooked thorns.[45] Tenacity is just as remarkable. Hammada (*Haloxylon salicornicum*) stubbornly adheres to even mobile sheets of sand,[46] and Shortleg Bushmen Grass (*Stipagrostis scoparia*) requires such a mobile substrate for growth and establishment.[47] Broomtree (*Retama raetam*) remains alive even when its roots are exposed or its crown covered with sand.[48]

Biblical authors would have known the desert was harsh, dangerous, and uncompromising (Ps 107,4–9).[49] The biblical wilderness is not Walden Pond; as Bill Bryson points out, true wilderness terrified even Thoreau.[50] In modern studies of wilderness experience, the danger—especially the unknown danger of the wilderness—is one of the most significant experiential aspects subjects noted.[51] For biblical writers, the desert was unknown, unmapped (Ps 107,4.33; Jer 51,43), much of it unnamed, evoking "an elusive hint of something unknown, unknowable, about to be revealed".[52] The desert is immense, immeasurable,—too immense for human beings[53].

On the other hand, the deserts of Midian, Edom, and the Negev are technically *bādia*, not *ṣaḥārā*, that is, not entirely sand, except for a few parts of the Sinai Peninsula. *Bādia* is capable of growing vegetation and even of cultivation—barley, sorghum, cantaloupe—when the winter rains send torrents streaming down the wadis.[54] Perennial plants grow wherever ground water is available within cracks in the hard rock.[55] Artemisia shrubs abound in the furrows that cut across the gravelly slopes of the wadis, even growing in patches on open sand where seeping underground water sustains them, and they are edible and widely grazed.[56] Thorny acacia produces a gum that can be dissolved in water to treat eye infections and jaundice; its seeds pulverized treat diarrhea;

The Corporal Desert

the bark can treat asthma.[57] When the rains of March come, the desert blooms into color (Ps 113,9),[58] with flowers such as the red anemone, "a brilliant scarlet . . . the most gorgeously painted, the most conspicuous in spring, the most universally spread of all the floral treasures of the Holy Land".[59] Fauna, too, abound: the habitat diversity of small mammals in the Negev is high compared to other deserts.[60] Thus, Al-Maqrizi (c. 1400) reports that the Caliph Umar said he asked Rabbi Kaʿab al-Aḫbar about the world and received the answer: "When God created things, he made for each a partner. . . . Hardship said, 'I am setting out for the desert', and Salubrity said, 'And I go with you'".[61] Or, as the theologian Gisbert Greshake writes, "O gilt wirklich beides: Die Wüste ist schön *und* die Wüste ist schrecklich".[62.]

IV

PARTICIPANT OBSERVATION

Participant Observation

WHEN WE SPEAK OF THE EFFECT OF LANDSCAPE ON THE BODY, on the human eye, we are being phenomenological.[1] "The key issue in any phenomenological approach is the manner in which people experience and understand the world."[2] Matthew Johnson dismisses such approaches to landscape as Romanticism, "about opening one's heart and mind and simply seeing (or sensing)",[3] but as the archaeologist Christopher Tilley writes, "Knowledge of place stems from human experiences, feeling and thought".[4] Bourdieu is ambivalent: he argues that "native theories" are dangerous because they reinforce scholars' own predispositions, such as setting up principles of production as norms governing practice.[5] On the other hand, he nevertheless rejects functional approaches that bracket "the agents' own representation of the world and of their practice".[6] We therefore need to follow the anthropologists in engaging in participant observation.[7] For this reason, some verbatim statements of those who have reflectively written on desert experiences are valuable.[8]

Edward Abbey worked for two years as a ranger for the United States National Park Service at Arches National Monument near Moab, Utah, writing a memoir of his experiences in his 1968 book, *Desert Solitaire*. One of his first observations was "the immense silence in which I am lost".[9] Many writers note this silence in particular.[10] As Huxley wrote, the "Silence of the desert is such that casual sounds . . . cannot abolish it. They co-exist with it".[11] Baudrillard expands on this into the realm of sight: "The silence of the desert is a visual thing, too. A product of the gaze that stares out and finds nothing to reflect it".[12]

Theatre critic, naturalist, nature writer, and an early conservationist Joseph Wood Krutch lived in the Arizona desert from 1952 to his death in 1970. He highlights the power of the blazing sun: "Under the open sky the sun's rays strike with an almost physical force".[13] Yet Krutch also speaks of the desert as filled with life. He writes, "The desert is sprinkled with hundreds, probably thousands, of evenly placed shrubs, varied now and then by a small tree", including the acacia abundant in the deserts of Edom and Midian.[14] As in Edom and Midian, "All the little annual flowers and weeds which spring up after the winter rains and rush from seed to seed again in six weeks gave up the ghost at the end of their short lives".[15] Yet as we have said for Israelite writers, the flora and fauna that are adapted to the desert's special geography and climate are twisted and outlandish because of that environment.[16]

Although Krutch's "participant observation" is that of a naturalist, it has by the end of *The Voice of the Desert* moved to the sublime. He reflects on the biological anecdotes he has provided in his memoir and then asks why he has not asked, "Who cares"? or "So what"? He replies, "The ultimate answer, I think, is to be found only by admitting the mystical element. The reason for my deepest caring does not lie within the scope of biology or even metabiology. One cannot recognize it without being to that extent a mystic".[17]

Participant observation, however, ordinarily means the researcher's own observations, "face-to face relationship with the observed . . . thus, the observer is part of the context being observed, and he both modifies and is influenced by this context".[18] Timothy Insoll, one of the foremost archaeologists of religion, is wary of invoking our own experiences and perceptions, wary that it will become essentialist and ethnocentric.[19] But in so doing, Insoll condemns any cognitive science approach to the past, and does so explicitly.[20] Participant observation is necessary to avoid being "systematically deaf to the distinctive tonalities of [Israelite] existence".[21] The goal "is not to achieve some sort of inner correspondence of spirit with" the ancient Israelite, but "to figure out what the devil they think they are up to".[22] With a mix of diffidence and temerity, therefore, I have approached the desert—sc. the Deep Negev—myself. I have chosen a

Participant Observation

dérive as the best method for psychogeographical analysis, which merits discussing its background and procedures. The English discipline of Psychogeography stems from Guy Debord's *dérive*,[23] a practice invented by Debord's Lettrist movement, itself an offshoot of Situationism.[24] Debord's goal with the *dérive* was the "Study of the precise laws and specific effects of the geographical environment, consciously organized or not, on the emotions",[25] and it had an explicit activist agenda.[26] The *dérive* has since been repeatedly accepted, rejected, and popularized again and again.[27] In the 1990s, the movement known as Mythography began to consciously move *dérives* away from the performances they had become.[28] Mythographers focused increasingly on liminal spaces.[29] At the same time, *dérives* Debord had intended as group activities became increasingly solitary.[30] Mythography also incorporated study of the mythology of a landscape,[31] and, in so doing, came to resemble so-called Goethean Science (to which we shall return),[32] because, as we have seen, space becomes a canvas for inscribing memories.[33] Contrariwise—and this is why I chose this method—memories can be accessed by *dérive*-ing,[34] since memory is materialized in the landscapes.[35]

Independent of these developments, the geographer Gilbert White and the psychologist Kevin Lynch coined the term "Psychogeography," adopted along with their definition by the geographer Robert Kates and psychologists Joachim Wohlwill and David Stea at Clark University.[36] Their form of Psychogeography was also about psycho-sensual effects and impressions of landscape,[37] about unities of ambience floating in spaces.[38]

My *dérive*, however, adopts the methodological steps of Goethean Science. That is, it is mutual interaction with the phenomenon of the landscape,[39] especially sensual interaction,[40] how the landscape catches attention,[41] and what happens during the encounter.[42] On a basic level, it is walking or otherwise traversing a landscape, while emotions focus attention on certain features.[43] "Walking increases creative ideation".[44] The route suggests itself,[45] drawing the researcher by attractions of the terrain.[46] It is therefore *not* random, not the random arbitrary wanderings attempted by the Surrealists, which Debord called "imbecilities."[47] The *dérive* is "rapid",[48] but practiced by varying speed,[49] even standing still at times.[50] The researcher ignores signage and the movement of other people,[51] and follows "vortexes that strongly encourage entry into or exit from certain zones",[52] "paths of least resistance".[53] "Above all, the dominating action of centers of attraction" need to be noted.[54] This beginning of the 'drift' is what Goethean Science calls "Exact Sensory Perception",[55] taking a many-sided epitome of the phenomenon.[56]

The researcher writes down sights and sounds without judgment or evaluation.[57] This act is Johann Wolfgang Goethe's "Exact Sense Perception." One can also sketch maps or diagrams.[58] The researcher writes while walking as well as while pausing.[59] The written/drawn representations are Goethe's "Exact Sensorial Imagination",[60] an exact fashioning of an exemplification,[61] including emotional affect.[62] The final stage is seeing the whole, seeing connections.[63] Such ethnographic experience then has to be rendered into narrative.[64]

Since passive-voice description only pretends to disguise the authorial presence,[65] it seems best to state that "I undertook" a *dérive* of several regions of the desert South in February 2017 that confirms many of the same perceptions of other observers, and I provide here only the final connections. One of my first and strongest observations was silence (especially in the Deep Negev), and as Huxley says the sparse, thin bird sounds do not eliminate the silence (in Edom, for instance).[66] The few sounds one does hear seem to travel for great distances (in the Deep Negev). It is also an olfactory silence, as smells are peculiarly absent. Wind is distinctly present (in Edom, Midian), or rather, one notices the wind in an exceptional way, both aurally and physically. When the wind ceases, one is struck by the stillness of everything—a silence of motion (noticeable in the Kadesh Barnea area). The sense of endlessness, of vast emptiness, is not hindered by mountains that cut the horizon (e.g., in Midian, as presented below).[67]

The point of this exercise, again, is "not . . . imagining myself as someone else," but as an adjunct to "searching out and analyzing the symbolic forms—words, images, institutions, behaviors—in terms of which, in each place, people actually represent themselves to themselves and to one another".[68]

V

DESERT WIND

Desert Wind

GOD IS NOT MERELY THE DESERT, but in Zechariah 9 a desert storm, the unforgettable *Khamsin* or Sirocco of the desert and its accompanying sand storms.[1] It is the south wind, in fact, that is especially feared in the Levant (Jer 13,24; Isa 21,1–2; Job 37,17),[2] and one of its names is *Jibli*, or "south".[3] As Jer 4,11 says, "A searing wind blows from the barren heights in the wilderness". Isa 21,1 speaks of "the whirlwinds of the Negev." "The winds . . . are quite often devastating and have penetrated so deep into the consciousness of the inhabitants".[4] In the Talmud, Abba Arikha claims that four winds blow each day, and the South is the harshest of them all; if it were not for the angel Ben Neitz who blocks it, it would destroy the entire world (*b. Git.* 31b, on the basis of Job 39,26).

The Khamsin is a meteorological phenomenon common from February to May and can last up to three or even seven days.[5] While in Jonah, the Khamsin is an east wind because the scene is in Mesopotamia, in the Levant the Khamsin originates in Arabia and reaches Palestine dry and with high-speed winds.[6] The barometric pressure plummets.[7] When it arrives, visibility is greatly impaired, and the sky turns yellow or red.[8] The low humidity has its own effects, as the winds "desiccate the landscape, wither leaves and fruit on trees, render the brush vegetation susceptible to fires".[9] The winds stir up sandstorms quickly, whirlwinds to tremendous heights engulfing foliage and scouring up the soil.[10] T.E. Lawrence (Lawrence of Arabia) writes from his own experience, "At last I saw that part of the yellow cloud . . . was coming slowly against the wind in our direction, raising scores of dust devils before its feet. The cloud was nearly as high as a hill".[11] "The sparse vegetation withers and is choked by the great quantities of sand and dust carried by these winds".[12] The heat is almost unbearable;[13] Lawrence writes, "The heat steadily increased with an oppression and sultriness which took me by surprise. I kept turning my head to see if some mass was not just behind me, shutting off the air".[14] Breathing becomes difficult, akin to what one experiences at high altitude.[15]

For more extended firsthand witness, we have Wasfi Zakariya's description from *'Ashāir al-Shām*:

> Between heaven and earth rage the whirlwinds and sandstorms of the desert, whirling like a pillar of tremendous heat and stirring up a tempest of dust and soil.... You can see it approaching from the bowels of the sandy waste or the heart of the desert steppe, at first almost resembling a line drawn across the horizon, then rising and swelling into the air, its winds intensifying to driving blasts that carry the soil and dust away, whirling it along the ground and lifting it up into the air.... It appears like a wall towering to the clouds in the sky, soaring, surging and looming closer, and then suddenly it engulfs you and plunges you into a dark cloud, a deep sullen shimmering red.[16]

Or again, Lawrence:

> The sun disappeared, blotted out by thick rags of yellow air over our heads. We stood in a horrible light, ochreous and fitful. The brown wall of cloud from the hills was now very near, rushing changelessly upon us with a loud grinding sound. Three minutes later it struck, wrapping us in a blanket of dust and stinging grains of sand, twisting and turning in violent eddies, and yet advancing eastward at the speed of a strong gale. We had put our camels' backs to the storm, to march before it: but these internal whirling winds tore our tightly-held cloaks from our hands, filled our eyes, and robbed us of all sense of direction.[17]

VI

THE TEXTUAL DESERT

The Textual Desert

LET US RETURN NOW TO THE TEXT, to the literary desert in the literary South, since, as we have seen, language can "superimpose abstractions onto concrete reality".[1] Nevertheless, literature can also "lift the veil of familiarity", as J. R. R. Tolkien says, on location by imaginative wording.[2] The way in which the Bible speaks of the desert South provides a specific evoking of that place.[3] Because mythic language operates on the level of semantic domains, rather than with isolated terms,[4] it will be helpful to look at the semantic domains of the words that describe the places implicated,[5] both first for the pure form "South", and then for the more widely distributed related motif complex "Desert".[6]

Hebrew has at least three different systems of terminology for direction, depending on the perspective from which the writer is operating, and these are attested in Ugaritic, as well.[7] Building on the work of Michael O'Connor,[8] Wyatt designates these the Homuncular/Religious, Topographical, and Cosmological/Solar, and only the former two have designations for "South".[9] The Homuncular or Religious set includes *yamin*, lit. "right", and its derivative *teman* in Hebrew and *ymn* in Ugaritic. The Topographical uses both *negeb* and *darom* in Hebrew, with no Ugaritic counterparts. Wyatt notes that only the Homuncular set is complete for all directions in Ugaritic and is common to both languages, concluding that it is the older vocabulary.[10] This oldest category is a set of terms related to aspects of the body, terms such as "right [hand]" for South, while the Topographical category supplements the Homuncular with more objective, neutral terms belonging to geographic features.[11]

This reinforces the value of the embodied meanings of geographic terms discussed above. As Tilley writes, "The human body provides the fundamental mediation point between thought and the world".[12] In that discussion, focus was on the desert, which is primary in how Israel perceived the mythic South. But in concert with the cognitive science perspective employed here, Wyatt discusses scholarship on the predominance of left-side cradling of infants nursing that has led scientists to conclude that "for the infant, security is experienced on the right side,"[13] and this has been confirmed in more recent studies.[14] "There would be enormous pressure, at first biological selectivity, and later cultural conformity, for behavioural conventions of the kind which would reinforce . . . the symbolic potential associated with each dimension, as in the use of [left] hands for toilet and [right for] eating functions, in ritual contexts and in general social interaction".[15] Wyatt also notes that anthropologists have identified right-handedness as early as Oldowan hammer stones.[16]

The conclusion to be drawn is that if South is "right", it ought to naturally be symbolic of security, "of well-being, of everything ordered".[17] Wyatt, however, notes that in spite of this, Northwest Semitic mythology associated the gods with the North, including Yahweh in Ps 48,3, an association that only highlights the "alternative tradition which has Yahweh proceeding from Teman (sc. the south)".[18] This paradox therefore stands alongside the animosity toward Edom and Midian as evidence of the mythic importance of having Yahweh come from the South.

Teman, however, is used solely in a directional sense only in the Pentateuch. In other passages, it can be a proper place name (Job 2,11; Ezek 25,13; &c.), regularly associated with wise inhabitants (Job 2,11; 15,18; Bar 3,22–23—as was Edom *apud* Jer 49,7),[19] or it can be translated "South Wind". In contrast to *darom*, *teman* South Wind does not have negative connotations. In Ps 78,26, it is neutral, while in Song 4,16 it is the wind that blows on the beloved's garden and spreads fragrance. Such a desert wind Kerry Walters describes, with allusions to the Hebrew and Greek terms *ruah* and *pneuma*: "Desert air grows pellucid and fragrant with the presence of the great nothingness which is God".[20]

Darom, with no convincing etymology,[21] likewise has both a directional sense, as in Ezekiel, and the meaning "South Wind". In Job 37,17, the *Darom* South Wind brings dreadful heat on the land, an understanding for the South Wind found also in Luke 12,55, where the Syriac has *Teman*.

Negeb derives from a verbal meaning of "to cleanse" or "to wipe". Because of this etymology, the South becomes in Jewish tradition the "direction of *teshuvah* [repentance]",[22] *Negeb* refers to all Israel's southern lands south of the Hebron downland.[23]

The same terms are variously translated "desert" or "wilderness" by English versions. The word *midbar* is derived from the root *DBR* in the meaning of "back, remote" (cf. Akk *duppuru*),[24] and is normally generic: only 24 of its 217 occurrences are qualified by a geographical name.[25] *Midbar* is most often used in the context of the Exodus and the subsequent years of testing (Deut 2,14–16; Numbers 1–25).[26] Secondarily, it appears in prophetic passages anticipating redemption through the wilderness. In Ps 75,6, it has a directional sense, as the context is "East, West, or desert". There are, however, a number of descriptive passages. In these, the *midbar* is described literally as arid (2 Sam 17,27–29; 2 Kgs 3,8–9; Pss 107,3–4.35; Isa 35,6; 41,18; 50,2; Jer 17,6), uninhabited (Job 38,26; Jer 17,6), without plant life (Gen 36,24; 1 Sam 17,28; Jer 2,2; 12,12; 2 Chron 26,10; Job 24,5; Sir 18,19), or only thorns (Judg 8,7), inhabited by snakes, scorpions, and owls (Deut 8,15; Jer 2,24; Ps 102,6), along with human fugitives (Hagar, Moses, Elijah, David, &c.). Figuratively, the *midbar* is "barren, howling" (Deut 32,10) and "great and terrible" (Deut 8,15).[27] It is noted for its wind (Deut 32,10; Jer 13,24; Prov 21,19).

When Moses and Aaron appear before Pharaoh, they ask permission to journey three days into the *midbar* to worship God (Exod 3,18; 5,1.3; 7,16; 8,27–28). No mountain is mentioned here. Significantly, then, although what happens in the narrative is not a three-day worship trip but an emigration, the notion is not of journeying to Mount Sinai to meet God but journeying to the *midbar* to meet God, which is exactly what Exod 16,10 says happens.

The term *tsiyya* is used only for the testing of the Israelites in the wilderness, although it is only found in postexilic prophetic and poetic books (e.g., Isa 25,5; 32,2).[28] *Jeshimon* appears for both the Wilderness testing period and for predictions of future redemption through the wilderness. Its root is *YŠM*, "to be desolate".[29] *Arabah*, which is often a proper place name for the Jordan Rift Valley south of the Dead Sea, is typically translated as "desert" or "wilderness" in several passages, particularly in predictions of redemption through it. In Jer 5,6 it is the domain of the wolf, while in Jer 51,43, it is arid and uninhabited, "arid ... land where no one lives, where no human being even passes through" (CSB)—exactly as Baudrillard claims: "The grandeur of the desert derives from their being, in their aridity, the negative of the earth's surface and of our civilized humors".[30] *Arabah* lacks any of the positive associations that sometimes accompany *midbar*.[31]

If we are going to consider semantics, however, it is important to examine how the "desert" or "south" appears in the poetic texts of Deuteronomy 33, Judges 5, Psalm 68, Habakkuk 3, and Zechariah 9 mentioned earlier. In each of those fragments, the final terms indicate the place name from which God "comes". Some of these are nouns that refer to places: the South, the desert, his clifftop sanctuary, his southland mountain slopes. The rest are proper toponyms: Seir, Mount Paran, and Edom. In each case, the term serves an identical semantic and syntactical function in the passage.

As Keith Basso enjoins, we begin "by examining some of the statement[s]'s linguistic features, focusing attention on the morphology and semantics of its several primary tropes.

We then move on to consider the internal logic".[32] We cannot go straight from form to get at content.[33] One could discuss the poetic passages' syntactic, semantic usage using a very specific and technical way of dealing with language based on the predictability of syntactic combinations, like Minimal Recursion Semantics or Head-driven Phrase Structure Grammar. Those theories, however, are not very convincing semantically or for discourse analysis, and the cost-benefit of learning to use those models is devastating as they are closed systems and change a lot depending on the authors.[34]

Enunciative Linguistics provides better tools. Enunciative linguistics examines the distinctions between the individual employment of language, or *l'énonciation*, and the linguistic artifacts resulting from this employment, or *l'énoncé*.[35] This is not the same as the longstanding *langue / parole* distinction, which goes back to Saussure.[36] Saussure's distinction is between pre-existent abstract, systematic rules and conventions of a signifying system (*langue*) and the concrete instances of its use (*parole*). On the other hand, *l'énonciation*, although it can be thought of as a system, is a shared mental catalogue, a collective ideational corpus, *out of which* speakers and writers draw a single intended usage that is also comprehended by their listeners or readers—although multiplicity of senses may be part of that intended use.[37] Thus, syntactic conditions, semantics, and pragmatics are all aspects of *l'énonciation*,[38] and all of these in the particulars of cultural context.[39]

Therefore, we first focus in our poetic fragments on the use of defined descriptions and proper names.[40] The definite article is not incidental. By speaking of *the* desert, *the* south, the text assumes the hearer and reader of these passages is capable of identifying the desert in question, that they know something about the south.[41] This specificity permits discussing the actual Negev and Arabian deserts to explain the biblical image intended. The proper names, as well, can

The Textual Desert

be employed only if the interlocutor is supposed to know to what they refer, at least partially: Seir, Mount Paran, and Edom.[42]

Moving to wider context, the desert/wilderness is used in multiple ways in the Hebrew Bible.[43] The first of these is resoundingly negative, the desert as a sort of hell (Joel 2, 1–3; Isa 21,1; 34,13–14; Lam 5,9; also 4QApocrLamA 1.1.12; 1QM [War Scroll] 1.2, 3),[44] just as in Ugaritic texts it is the abode of Mot, Death (KTU 1.4 vii.55–57). This sense is behind the sending of the Azazel goat covered in Israel's sins into the desert on the Day of Atonement. The śā'îr of Lev 17,7; Isa 13,21; 34,14, the Lilith of Isa 34,4, and the flying serpents of Isa 30,6 are the desert's demonic denizens (possible, too, the *yemim* of Gen 36,24).[45]

A similar view is found in cuneiform literature, where the same words are used for the desert as for the netherworld: *ki-erṣetu* and *kur-šadu*.[46] Laura Feldt has analyzed the image of wilderness in the interrelated myths of Inanna, Ninurta, Lugalbanda, and Gilgamesh, "some of the most detailed Mesopotamian sources on the theme of wilderness".[47] In these narrative texts, the Old Babylonian wilderness is a fearsome land of terrors (*Inanna and Ebih*, 116–20, 127–30; *Lugalbanda in the Mountain Wilderness*, 151–70; *Lugalbanda and Anzu*, 1–5) that nevertheless by the action of heroes can be transformed and organized into a source of plenty (*LugalE*, 347–67; *Inanna and Ebih*, 121–26; *Lugalbanda in the Mountain Wilderness*, 265–325).[48] However, this more positive view of the wilderness in Mesopotamia, unlike Israel, may be because urban areas were "fundamentally dependent upon interaction with and travel into wilderness areas".[49] Moreover, outside of the narrative genre the tenor is far more negative: in magic texts, for example, the steppe is the domain of demons and exorcists address the desert demons oppressing their patients.[50] *Madbaru* is a "place of hunger and thirst" (Assurbanipal), "where there are no wild animals" (Assurbanipal)[51]. Ḫuribtu is "uninhabited" (Ashurnirari VI), a place of ghosts (eṭemmu; KAR 184).[52]

A second sense, or perhaps a version of the first, is the Wilderness as a place of trial, in particular the time of testing during the Wilderness Wanderings of the Israelites after the Exodus (e.g., Deut 1–3; 9,1–10,11; Ezek 20,10ff).[53] The most thoroughgoing study of this sense is Terry Burden's 1994 monograph.[54] It is noteworthy that Deuteronomy, primarily about this Wilderness testing, is framed by the Decalogue of Deut 5,7–11 and the hymn of Deuteronomy 32 plus the blessing in Deuteronomy 33, which is introduced by the poetic passage listed above.

Although the Wilderness Wanderings draw on the negative connotations of the desert, a tradition holds that very period was a time of closeness to God (Deut 32,10–11; 1 Kings 19; Jer 2,2.6; Mic 6,4; Am 2,9; Hos 2,14–15; Ps 55,7–8).[55] The Wilderness is the place where the Law, the covenant, the sanctuary, and the festivals originated.[56] Perhaps this lies behind the refrain of Song 3,6 and 8,5: "Who is this coming up from the desert"?[57] Or the emphasis there may be on the solitude of the desert.[58] In any case, the idea of the Wilderness Wanderings as a time of closeness with God is still dependent on the setting being an actual desert. The desert environment serves as a contrast to the "fleshpots of Egypt" (Num 11,1–6), as well as to the rains, fertility, and agriculture associated with the god Baal (Hos 2,16–17; 13,5).[59] The use of the desert as a particular form of punishment for sin is therefore dependent on it being both a place of closeness to God and of testing (Ezek 47,9–10).[60]

Because of its significance as a place of meeting God and because of its solitude, the desert becomes a place to which people go for contemplation (1 Kgs 19,3–4; 2 Kgs 4,38–39; Jer 9,2). Elijah and Elisha are most notable, here, but Jeremiah opines, "I wish I had a lodging place in the desert

The Textual Desert

where I could spend some time like a weary traveler" (Jer 9,2).

Nevertheless, as we have seen, there is another usage of the desert, and that is the association in the poetic fragments discussed above of God himself with the desert, the desert being the domain of the divine, the source of Yahweh's horizontal theophany.[61]

VII

The Folkloric Desert

The Folkloric Desert

AGAIN, HOWEVER, TO UNDERSTAND THE LITERARY OR MYTHIC DESERT ultimately from a cognitive perspective, it is worth looking at how the desert appears as a mythic theme in folklore more broadly.[1] The link between folklore and cognitive science is indebted to exploration by Mircea Eliade, Stith Thompson, Vladimir Propp, Edmund Leach, Morton Fried, and Carl Jung of how throughout history and around the world, human beings make the same myths and tales.[2]

Jung famously associated these recurrent motifs with his, at times, vaguely defined archetypes.[3] Although Jung did not introduce the term until 1919, he began discussing the idea behind it in 1912.[4] For Jung, the archetype is a natural human predisposition toward a specific image, images such as the desert or wilderness more generally.[5] Thus, the archetype is not the image itself but, as Martin Lings writes, "The Archetype is always the heir who inherits back the symbol in which it manifests Itself".[6] Jung did *not* think that the images could be inherited.[7] Nevertheless, all symbolism depends at least slightly on the prior archetypes.[8]

Erik Goodwyn has investigated *why* certain stories recur and others do not, "Why is one story fascinating, memorable and evocative . . . but the other comes across as mere noise? Why does one story spontaneously show up everywhere, but another hardly ever emerge"?[9] In our case, why the desert, which is unquestionably such an archetype?[10] Following Dan Sperber, Goodwyn argues that the answer is cognitive, that "cross-culturally recurrent features of human minds inform and constrain".[11] Unconscious psychological processes cause humans to imagine and tell stories that converge, over generations of storytelling, on what folklorists called—without explaining causality—indexable motifs and tale types.[12] In this way, cultural narratives play a role in translating cognitive material and "unconscious thought" into coherent orientations toward places,[13] but those cultural narratives themselves are over time reinforced according to cognitive

The Folkloric Desert

forces. Those diachronic self-correcting convergences have noticeable tendencies, among which Goodwyn lists: "Environments that are also general, but simple and easy to visualize".[14] Certainly, the desert wilderness is such a case.[15] What is more, what he calls "highly resonant expressions" include those that "will be emotionally evocative, perhaps stimulating . . . the convergent affective systems involving fear . . . seeking, and hunger".[16] "Resonant expressions should be sensually vivid and clearly defined . . . clearly defined and vivid environments that are simple and not overburdened with descriptors, yet not overly abstract either".[17]

Goodwyn presents this as prediction, "hypothecated without reference to evidence" and "invite[s] clinicians and researchers to test these predictions".[18] The mythic desert bears them out. In other words, biblical authors did not choose the image of the desert out of the blue, but because it mapped onto existing cultural understanding, it supported the mythology that was already there.[19] This means one can also reverse Goodwyn's procedure, and proceed not from the workings of the mind to the most fit motifs, but back from the motif to an understanding of the mind, as is being done here.[20] So our interest lies in the wilderness archetype, the wilderness as motif in folklore in general: landscapes holding in common attributes into which the desert can be resolved,[21] since it is precisely on those common attributes that the metaphorical, symbolic capacity of the desert operates.[22] That wilderness need not always be a desert; wildernesses function similarly whether they are desert, inaccessible mountains, or, to a large extent, even the sea in a non-seafaring society.[23] The particulars of a desert were important in the Israelite mythic vernacular, as we have seen, but now that we have moved to comparative literature, other sorts of wildernesses should be considered.

As Worman has shown, not all cultures have a wilderness archetype. Worman determines if dominant wilderness

The Folkloric Desert

archetypes exist by looking for a number of mentions of wilderness that exceed Peirce's Criterion Limit and where the wilderness described in the folk tales matches a region with a high Ruggedness Index.[24] German and Korean folklores have the archetype; Irish does not.[25] What constitutes a wilderness varies: forest for German, mountains for Korean, but the function in folklore is the same.[26] Factors that favor the presence of a wilderness archetype in a culture include rugged native terrain, an economy strongly influenced by terrain, and links to other cultures with a wilderness archetype.[27] Once such an archetype has arisen in folklore, this fact discourages development within the wilderness in the future.[28]

In the Ancient Near East, in addition to what has been said above about the wilderness in Akkadian literature, Hittite texts make the steppe the domain of supernatural beings (*KUB* 8.71; 7.14).[29] In Egyptian literature, the desert is a terrifying place in the *Tale of Sinuhe* (B 231–32).[30] At the same time, it is a source for riches: silver, gold, and lapis lazuli (*Urk.* 4.501; Papyrus Boulaq 17 8.6–7).[31]

The *Odyssey* assigns the cyclops to the "high mountains" (9.112–14).[32] Homer also refers to the centaurs as *oreskoioisi,* or "mountain-bred" (*Iliad* 1.267–68).[33] A Greek curse likens the mountains to the sea, both places from which no return was possible.[34]

In Islamic folklore, "the desert is 'wondrous' because it harbors the supernatural, which can be deadly: for example, the desert is the abode of malevolent djinn who enjoy laying traps for humans or driving them mad".[35] In Arabic poetry, the desert is the place of danger, hunger, thirst, and loneliness.[36] The primary term for wilderness in Quranic Arabic is ʿarāʾ, from a root meaning "naked".[37]

A "Great Wilderness" features in the Chinese myth, *Classic of Mountains and Seas* or *Shan Hai Jing* (second century BC). There are repeated references to mountains "in the middle of the Great Wilderness", at almost each of which the sun and moon are said to rise (books 14–17).[38] Among the fantastic peoples who live on these mountains are gods and shamans.[39] Distinct from the Great Wilderness is the vast desert, Flowing Sands, which also contains mountains inhabited by gods.[40]

In India, the polarity attested in myth, epic, law, and medicine is between the village (*grāma*) and forest (*araṇya*), between dry land (*jāṅgala*) and the marshy (*anūpa*), whose overgrown mangrove forests assumed the wilderness role (*Taittirīya-Saṃhitā* 5.4.9.1; 6.1.8.1; 7.2.2.1; *Vājasaneyi-Saṃhitā* 3.45; *Śatapatha-Brāhmaṇa* 2.5.2.20ff).[41] This rain forest was "full of troubles" (Charaka, *Charaka Saṃhitā* 3.47–48; Vāghbaṭa, *Aṣṭāṅgasaṅgraha* 3.79),[42] and "many dangers" (*Panchatantra* 1.10, 155)[43]. The word for forest, *araṇya*, derives from *araṇa*, "strange".[44] It is associated with the Aeolian gods Rudra and Vayu (*Taittirīya-Āraṇyaka* 3.11–12).[45] Nevertheless, it was to this wilderness that the "renouncer" (*sannyāsin*) retired in the last stage of his life for contemplation, akin to the Anthonian desert of the early Christians (see below).[46]

The 13th-century Prose (Younger) *Edda* of Snorri Sturluson provides the most complete survey of Norse mythology. Its wilderness is the mountains. The mountains, including the East of Scandinavia and the interior of Iceland, are repeatedly attested as the domain of the giants (and later, trolls, see opposite): in the Eddic poem *Hárbarðsljóð*,[47] in *Gylfaginning* 22–23, in words of Úlfr Uggason's *Husdrapa* quoted in *Skáldskaparmál* 4, and in Thiodolf of Hvinir's *Haustlöng* quoted in *Skáldskaparmál* 17.[48] The Saga *Heimskringla* claims that wise men sent by the king of Denmark to explore Iceland found the mountains full of nature spirits (*landvættir*).[49] Legal and historical literature agreed: the Medieval *Landnámabók* and the earlier *Ulfljótslög* speak of *bergbuar*, "rock inhabitants".[50] Not all

The Folkloric Desert

the wilderness's inhabitants were horrible, however; the *álfar*, elves, similar to humans but fairer and wiser, with greater spiritual powers, keener senses, and a deeper understanding of nature[51]—only after the thirteenth century do they merge with the nature spirits and eventually "fairy-ize".[52] The wilderness / civilization polarity, however, is blurred by archaeological evidence for intensive use of the mountains (in Norway, for instance) from the Neolithic to the present—in the Iron Age for metallurgy, just as in the Levant.[53] It was, therefore, as for the biblical South, a *known* wilderness, drawing on the experience of the desert rather than a "great unknown" beyond the boundaries of experience.[54] Such known wildernesses are "better articulated and more consciously held than mythical space of the [imaginary] kind".[55]

For Nilotic peoples, the wilderness is a place of transcendent experiences, where individuals undergo psychic raptures.[56] For their Bantu neighbors, the wilderness is out-of-bounds for humans, inhabited by beings of power that compete with humanity for control of territory.[57] The Bantu groups of Highland Kenya (Luhya, Kuria, Kikuyu, Kamba) consider the wilderness hill country sacred, but never a place of pilgrimage.[58] This sacredness invokes fear. Wild places should not be entered, except in large groups, and trespassing on them could unleash violent weather on human communities.[59]

Several desert or mountainous wildernesses feature in the folklore of American Indian groups. In several cases, as with the Norse myths and Bantu beliefs, humanoid figures of great power are said to inhabit these regions, although these entities are not as brutal as the Norse giants though they may be dangerous. In southcentral Alaska, "The Dena'ina and other Athabascans respond to the energized atmosphere of the mountains"[60] by locating "people" of power there.[61] The Shoshone envision dwarf- or leprechaun-like inhabitants of the Rocky Mountains,[62] although dead youths also play there.[63] For the Arapaho, the mountains of Wyoming are inhabited by Thunderbird Eagles,[64] and one is warned to avoid their mountain range, although the same mountains hold the Crow tribe's ceremonial fasting sites.[65] West Mitten Butte in Monument Valley (*Tsé Bii' Ndzisgaii*), Arizona, is for the Navajo home to a monster.[66] The Havasupai are too frightened to approach the San Francisco Peaks (*Wi:munakwa*) north of Flagstaff, Arizona, lest one stir up severe storms.[67]

The wind, too, has mythic importance, especially in Navajo thought, where it is associated with mountains and with cardinal directions as follows. Wind suffuses all nature, giving life, speech, thought, and motion.[68] Although all winds on earth are in actuality aspects of a single wind,[69] the four cardinal winds (i.e., North, South, East, and West) are the means by which the four mountains of the cardinal directions communicate with each other and apprehend and

The Folkloric Desert

direct happenings on earth.[70] "They [the winds] stand within the mountains, these [mountains] from then on being, by them, our sacred mountains".[71] This interface between cardinal direction, including South, (south) wind, and sacred mountain is fascinatingly congruent to what we have seen in the Hebrew Bible.

To unpack the spiritual experiences that shaped the text, the use of the desert archetype by spirituality throughout the centuries, read historically, is of great value, as it witnesses ongoing representations of that experience.[72] Beyond History of Interpretation or Reception History, therefore, which are post-exegetical, seeing what the mythic value of the desert archetype was for Abrahamic monotheists helps one understand the mythic intention of the biblical text.[73]

Let us begin this review of folklore with Jewish literature. "Desert" and "Wilderness" are prominent themes in both Midrashic and Kabbalistic traditions. If one uses as an arbitrary control corpus the collected works of Shakespeare, for instance, "desert/wilderness" has a relative frequency in Louis Ginzberg's *Legends of the Jews* of 4.5:1 over Shakespeare and of 8.2:1 for the Zohar. Interestingly, the peak of such terms' distribution in the Midrash is in the Exodus "Testing" material, while for the Zohar it is in the Joseph story. If one uses the terms for "desert" or "wilderness" as key words in context and works through the concordance entries as hits with context expanded, collocating clusters to see what is in proximity, the Midrash emphasizes the Exodus testing while the Zohar has just as much about the Azazel ritual on the Day of Atonement as it does the Exodus, thus emphasizing the liminal over the historical, the numinous over the legal.

The primary sense of desert in Jewish tradition is negative. It, like the sea, has an entrance to the netherworld, according to Jeremiah ben Eleazar (*b. Eruvin* 19a, based on Num 16,33). The Kabbalistic *Book of Bahir*, c. 1200 but with earlier traditions, describes the desert as an evil place of hunger and thirst (par. 161/107 in the Flavius Mithridates Latin edition, without Christian interpolations).[74]

In Jewish folklore, Midian and Edom are always the enemies of Israel. The only counter example is in Makhir ben Abba Mari's 14th-century *Yalqut ha-Makhiri*, which predicts that Elijah will meet the Messiah in the wilderness of Midian before the Messiah's manifestation and inauguration of the world to come (at Isa 11,4). This, then, emphasizes the desert as liminal place, a tenor that goes with the desert or wilderness in many folklores.

When the desert itself is referenced, as opposed to Midian the nation, the image is more positive. *Midrash Tanhuma* Deuteronomy 1 points out that the desert was a place of miracle making for Israel.[75] *Numbers Rabbah* 1.7 says that God revealed the Torah to Moses in the desert because the Torah had to be accompanied by fire, water, and desert, because all three belong to the human race.[76]

The desert archetype, although by no means a central image in mystic reflection,[77] has served several non-exclusive functions in the history of Christian spirituality.[78] Most familiar is desert as place to which ascetics flee and where they encounter God,[79] a usage that goes back to the Jewish Essenes (1QS [Community Rule] 9.19–20, building on the understanding of the desert as a place where the Torah can be rightly followed in CD 6.11, 18–20; 1QS 8.12–14; cf. Philo, *De Decalogo*, 10–11) and Therapeutae (Philo, *De Vita Contemplativa* 2.18–20).[80] Christian reflection on this Anthonian sense of desert, exemplified in the Desert Fathers (e.g., Athanasius, *Vita Antonii*; Jerome, *Vita Pauli*),[81] extends from the works of Origen[82] to Francis of Assisi on La Verna and Ignatius of Loyola's Manresa.[83] It is found in Sufi Islam (Rumi, *Masnavi* 6.2.459–62),[84] and is even the primary sense in which Jung understands the desert archetype.[85]

The Folkloric Desert

A second sense in Christian spirituality is the interior desert, a state of solitude and detachment where the Christian mentally communes with God.[86] Appearing first in Eucherius of Lyon's 5th-century *De laude heremi* (23, 39),[87] this is exemplified in Richard of St Victor (12th century) and Mechthild of Magdeburg (13th century)'s *Wüstunge*.[88] The inner desert is also a notion known to Sufi Islamic mysticism[89]. In Judaism, it is suggested by the Midrash in *Numbers Rabbah* 1.7: "If one cannot make oneself open and ownerless like the desert, one can acquire neither wisdom nor Torah".[90]

Yet the connotation of desert in Christian spirituality that comes closest to the desert God, the Yahweh of Teman, is not prominent until the later Middle Ages, especially with the Rhineland Mystics, a largely Dominican movement of speculative, apophatic spirituality. Meister Eckhart (d. 1327) popularized the desert as an image for God, using it more than a dozen times.[91] "God's desert is God's simple nature," he writes (*Tractate* 11).[92] For him, God is *Stille Wüste* (e.g., *Predigt* 10). The desert is God, or God is the desert, because of the desert's solitude (*Einöde*) (*Predigt* 10).

This sense of the mythic desert imaging God is picked up by Eckhart's disciple, Johannes Tauler (d. 1361), and Jan van Ruysbroeck (d. 1381). Tauler, for example, says God is "simple hidden desert (*Wüste*) beyond being" (*Sermon* 60). He highlights both the unknowability of God (*Predigt* 11; 55.5–7) and also God's "silent desert divinity" (*stille wüste Gottheit*; 278.3). Another of Eckhart's disciples, Henry Suso (d. 1366) speaks of the "*Weiselosigkeit*" of "desert deity" (*Wüste gotheit*).

The background of this understanding is twofold. The first is a strand that begins with Neo-Platonism. In the 3rd century, Plotinus borrowed the term used for the recess within the Delphic temple where the Pythia gave her oracles, called the *adyton* "not to slip in" or "beyond the image," to speak of the absolute spiritual beyond, surpassing visible reality (*Enneads*

The Folkloric Desert

VI.9.11).[93] By the end of the 5th century, *adyton* was for Simplicius of Cilicia, "the cloud of unknowing that the mystic encounters before the Ineffable One," and Damascius of Athens explained that its inaccessible character symbolized the transcendent ultimate, ineffable principle (*Difficulties and Solutions of First Principles* I.8.6–20). This usage had already found its way into Christian thought when Gregory of Nyssa used *adyton* to express the unknowability of God (*Life of Moses* 2.163–64).[94] Pseudo-Dionysius (c. 500) borrows directly from Neoplatonism, and *adyton* becomes in Latin *vastitas*, "wasteland."[95]

In the 9th century West, John Scotus Eriugena read Pseudo-Dionysius and made the desert wasteland the image of the divine.[96] In his commentary on the Gospel of John (1.27.80), Eriugena says, "The desert is the ineffability of the divine nature." When he goes on to say that the Greek word *erēmia* conveys the divine nature (*quod omnino diuinae coneunit naturae*; 1.27.85), he is echoing Pseudo-Dionysius (*Ecclesiastical Hierarchy* 3.7; *Divine Names* 4.24).[97] Eckhart and his school were reading Eriugena and perhaps Pseudo-Dionysius, as well, as when Van Ruysbroeck says, "We must all found our lives upon a fathomless abyss" (*Sparkling Stone*).[98]

On the other hand, the Eckhartian divine desert is a development from earlier Rhineland mystics who used the "Anthonian" understanding. Thus, van Rusybroeck draws on Pseudo-Hadewijch of Brabant (*Mengeldichten* 25–29), which draws on the authentic Hadewijch (*Mengeldichten* 1–16), both of which see the desert as a place to meet God, when he writes of "A wild, waste desert where God who loves us, lives" (van Ruysbroeck, *Werken* 3.217).[99] Van Ruysbroeck has taken the Anthonian desert and made it God's abode. But he also understands the desert and its "unconditioned dark" to be God (*Seven Degrees of Love*, chap. 14).

The Folkloric Desert

The desert as an image for the divine is thus uncommon in Christian spirituality, but present. It shows up in other monotheistic spiritual traditions on occasion. Thus, in the seventh of Baha'u'llah's "Seven Valleys" (1945) refers to the spiritual life as a quest for "This gazelle of the desert of oneness".[100]

VIII

Caveats

Caveats

IN TRYING TO UNDERSTAND WHAT DESERT MEANT TO THE BIBLICAL WRITERS, we must be wary of imposing what we think is common sense.[1] "Desert" is so familiar a notion that everyone has an image in their mind, although it in all probability derives from modern film and television and may not approach reality.[2]

Some participant observations succumb to this romantic, mawkish tendency. TED Talker and "Accidental Theologist" Lesley Hazleton's *Where Mountains Roar* muses about "beauty grasped not by the eyes but by the heart".[3] Or, "The desert can take us beyond what we think of as ourselves into another wider order of being", without explaining what that means.[4]

Things become even more untoward for the mythic desert when the deserts of the Middle East are envisioned. Western escapism becomes Orientalism and the desert an essential component of the exotic East of the 19th century.[5] But the problem is broader. As early as 1933, the Lakota leader Luther Standing Bear wrote about how the wilderness idea of virgin territory unsullied by man dispossessed those whose home it was.[6] What has been called the "Great Wilderness Debate" ignited when Ramachandra Guha published an essay in 1989 exposing how environmental protectionism dependent on the wilderness ideal erased indigenous peoples worldwide,[7] although ancient Israel never defined wilderness as empty of inhabitants but filled it with nebulous Ishmaelites, Amalekites, and the like. In the modern debate, environmentalists responded, and there were counter-rejoinders.[8] It has been argued that treating landscapes as "passive" objects of analysis is itself gendering them as feminine, thus engaging in sexism, as well.[9]

Nevertheless, it would be inaccurate to think the "desert mystique" is solely a Western construct, "that the cult of the wild is possible only in an atmosphere of comfort and safety and was therefore unknown to the pioneers who subdued half a continent".[10] Abbey cites the writings of multiple early cowboys, frontiersmen, and explorers whose experience of the wilderness was no different from his own.[11] In fact, the claim made by Edmund Burke in the eighteenth century and Ernest Renan in the 19th that the desert "breeds monotheists"[12] was first made by Islamic theologians, for whom the desert was a sort of deep freeze for isolated primitive monotheists, Hanifs preserving monotheism while the cities around them fell into polytheism in the centuries before Muhammed.[13] Some of these were thought to be isolated true followers of Jesus, uncorrupted by the Christian revisionism (e.g., Muqātil ibn Sulaymān [d. 767], *Tafsir* on Qur'an 57:27; Ibn Isḥaq [d. 767], *Sīrat Rasūl Allāh* on Zayd ibn Amr; Al-Tabari [d. 923], *Tafsir* on Qur'an 57:27),[14] but the focus is on the desert. As in John Cassian's *Conferences* (18.5), what enables monotheism to remain pure is the isolation and solitude of the desert experience.[15]

Of course, the desert does not "breed monotheists"; one need only look at pre-contact Australia to see this.[16] Abbey denies the desert necessarily leads one to God. Abbey writes, "God? I think, quibbling with Balzac; in Newcomb's terms, who the hell is *He*? There is nothing here, at the moment, but me and the desert. And that's the truth. Why confuse the issue by dragging in a superfluous entity"?[17] And yet, only a few pages later, Abbey is writing about "this desert vastness opening like a window onto eternity".[18]

IX

Conclusion

Conclusion

IF ISRAEL'S GOD IS THE DESERT GOD, he is strange, unfamiliar, and often fantastic.[1] God, Israel held, can be dangerous, as uncompromising as the desert,[2] and this is particularly true of how God appears in the desert (e.g., Exod 24,9–18; 33,18–34,8).[3] Danger and risk are essential elements of a desert God.[4] This God is unknown, unknowable *mysterium*,[5] but on the verge of being revealed (Exod 16,10; Song 8,5).[6] The desert God is formless and incorporeal as the desert is.[7] He is immeasurable, inestimable, the *Ein Sof* of Kabbalah.[8] As Aldous Huxley wrote, "Boundless and emptiness—these are the two most expressive symbols of that attributeless Godhead of whom all that can be said is St Bernard's *Nescio nescio*".[9] All the same, God is not malevolent, he "salubrious". The allusion is apt that Belden Lane draws in *The Solace of Fierce Landscapes* to a passage in C. S. Lewis's *The Lion, the Witch, and the Wardrobe*: Lucy asks regarding Aslan, the promised leonine king, "'Is he safe'? And Mr. Beaver, as honest as he is wise, responds, 'Who said anything about safe? 'Course he isn't safe! But he's *good!* He's the King, I tell you'".[10]

The desert silence, too, is a natural symbol of the divine, not—for Israel—in the sense of a God who does not speak, but a powerful, thick silence.[11] As Dickens wrote, "Listening to the intense silence is like looking at intense darkness" (*Bleak House*, chapter 58, "A Wintry Day and Night"). The biblical text, too, knows this silence: Ps 46,10: "Be still and know that I am God"; Hab 2,20: "Let all the world keep silent"; Ps 62,5: "Yet my soul, keep thou silence unto God"; Ps 65,1: "Praise is silent unto thee". Martha Robbins calls this the desert's "peace deeper than terror".[12]

The desert God, then, is an image that expresses a paradox. What Israel is trying to suggest is that Yahweh is a wild, wondrous God, enigmatic to the point of alien. Where God is not surreal, he is dangerous, the awful wind, soaring, surging, and looming.[13] The paradox is that the same God is

Conclusion

both "twisting and turning in violent eddies" and the "peace deeper than terror", tranquil and still as the motionless desert, dreadfully benevolent.

As Jung said, "We constantly use symbolic terms to represent concepts that we cannot define or fully comprehend".[14] They enable communicating concepts that cannot be communicated by other means.[15] Archetypes possess us, overwhelm us, because their corporeal encounter is vivid and momentous.[16] The staunchly anti-Jungian Jean Borella agrees: "Awareness of the sacred symbol is a disruptive and dazzling experience from which springs a consciousness of reality and the intellect . . . experience of the Transcendent within the experience of its sign's presence".[17]

Borella continues: "It is the archetype—or the metacosmic principle—of which signifier, meaning and particular referent are only distinct manifestations".[18] The mythic referent is where the corporeal image of the desert, its meanings as "solitary", "silent", "fierce", "beautiful", "unending", "strange", &c., and its mental forms of notions about God find their unique and unifying principle.[19] Or, as Ernst Cassirer wrote, the symbol or archetype presupposes that the ideas, in this case the myth, "are already given as definite quantities".[20]

Jean Szlamowicz writes, "The interplay between the literal meaning and the cultural roots" is the reason linguistic symbols "are still productive and so energetically compelling".[21] The desert South's continuing power to bear meaning and relevance is confirmed by such uses as Hosea Ballou II's 1837 hymn, "The mighty God from Teman came—The Holy One from Paran hill; His glory shone through heaven in flame, And all the earth his name did fill".[22] Of course, as that hymn alludes, Israel would never forget the desert South's association with the Exodus, Sinai, and the Law. There is, thus, an interplay of the liminal and the mimetic.[23] Nevertheless, the persistence of the desert

Conclusion

divinity alongside, and at times without, the divine desert, attests to the power of the cognitive, archetypical metaphor of Yahweh as a "desert God".

NOTES

Preface

1. As HEIDEGGER wrote (*The Piety of Thinking: Essays by Martin Heidegger*, trans. J. G. HART and J. C. MARALDO, Bloomington, Indiana University Press, 1976, pp. 10–11), "What is necessary for theology, therefore, can never be deduced from a purely rationally constructed system of sciences . . . The imparting of this revelation is not a conveyance of information about present, past, or imminent happenings; rather, this imparting lets one partake of the event which is revelation," all of which is beyond the scope of this study.
At the same time, it would be naïve to deny my own implicit ideology. All critical ethnographies are told from a vantage point, and one should be self-conscious of the voice in which the story is being told. Cf. L. BRODKEY, *Writing Critical Ethnographic Narratives*, in *Anthropology & Education Quarterly* 18 (1987) 67–76, pp. 68, 71.
2. See E. EKWEKE, *Can there be an African philosophy of science*, in *African Philosophy and the Hermeneutics of Culture*, ed. J. O. OGUEJIOFOR and G. I. ONAH (Studies in African Philosophy 2), Münster: LIT Verlag, 2005, p. 197.
3. V. Y. MUDIMBE, *Parables and Fables*, Madison: University of Wisconsin Press, 1991, p. 114.
4. T. OKERE, *African Philosophy: A Historico-hermeneutical Investigation of the Conditions of Its Possibility*, Lanham, MD: University Press of America, 1983, p. 12.
5. S. NGEWA, *God and His Creation Then and Now*, in *God and Creation*, ed. R. R. REED and D. K. NGARUIYA (Africa Society of Evangelical Theory series, 4), Carlisle: Langham, 2019, pp. 1ff.

6 M. MICHEL, *De l'herméneutique des symboles religieux*, in *Revue des Sciences Religieuses*, 49 (1975) 24–32, p. 32.

I
Introduction

1 R.D. MILLER II, *Yahweh: Origins of a Desert God* (Forschungen zur Religion und Literatur des Alten und Neuen Testaments, 284), Göttingen, Vandenhoeck & Ruprecht, 2021.
2 D. HYMES, *Foundations in Sociolinguistics*, Philadelphia, PA, University of Pennsylvania Press, 1974, p. 126.
3 G. GRESHAKE, *Eine Landschaft wie das Leben*, in *Publik-Forum Extra: Magazin für Spiritualität und Lebenskunst* 3 (October 2007) 19–21, p. 21.
4 On the way in which metaphoric language bears meaning and directs one's thinking, one of the best treatments remains C.S. LEWIS, *Bluspels and Flalansferes: A Semantic Nightmare*, in *Rehabilitations and Other Essays*, London, Oxford University Press, 1939; see also M. CHALEVELAKI, *Présence de l'objet et identité des marques de luxe*, PhD diss., Université Lumière Lyon 2, 2007, 6.1. Online: http://www.theses.fr/2007LYO20092; K.H. BASSO, *Wisdom Sits in Places: Landscape and Language among the Western Apache*, Albuquerque, NM, University of New Mexico Press, 1996, p. 40.
5 G. DAVENPORT, *The Geography of the Imagination: Forty Essays*, Boston, MA, David R. Godine, 2005, p. 4.
6 C.L. CRUMLEY, *Exploring the Venues of Social Memory*, in J. CLIMO – M.G. CATTELL (eds.), *Social Memory and History*, Walnut Creek, CA, Altamira, 2002, 39–52, pp. 41–42; BASSO, *Wisdom Sits in Places*, p. 66.
7 T. GUNNELL, *Nordic Folk Legends, Folk Traditions and Grave Mounds*, in E. HEIDE – K. BEK-PEDERSEN (eds.), *New Focus on Retrospective Methods: Resuming Methodological Discussions: Case Studies from Northern Europe* (Folklore Fellows' Communications, 307), Helsinki, Suomalainen Tiedeakatemia, Academia Scientiarum Fennica, 2014,

Notes to Introduction

17–41, pp. 23–24, 26, 31–32; Y. HELGASDÓTTIR, *Retrospective Methods in Dating Post-Medieval Rigmarole-Verses from the North Atlantic*, in E. HEIDE—K. BEK-PEDERSEN (eds.), *New Focus on Retrospective Methods: Resuming Methodological Discussions: Case Studies from Northern Europe* (Folklore Fellows' Communications, 307), Helsinki, Suomalainen Tiedeakatemia, Academia Scientiarum Fennica, 2014, 98–119, pp. 98–99; FROG, *Mythology in Cultural Practice: A Methodological Framework for Historical Analysis*, in *Retrospective Methods Network Newsletter* 10 (2015) 33–57, p. 34; D. SÄVBORG, *Scandinavian Folk Legends and Icelandic Sagas*, in E. HEIDE—K. BEK-PEDERSEN (eds.), *New Focus on Retrospective Methods: Resuming Methodological Discussions: Case Studies from Northern Europe* (Folklore Fellows' Communications, 307), Helsinki, Suomalainen Tiedeakatemia, Academia Scientiarum Fennica, 2014, 76–88, p. 85; M. EGELER, *A Retrospective Methodology for Using Landnamabok as a Source for the Religious History of Iceland?*, in *Retrospective Methods Network Newsletter* 10 (2015) 78–92, p. 81.

8   Y. BEREZKIN, *Folklore and Mythology Catalogue*, in *Retrospective Methods Network Newsletter* 10 (2015) 58–70, p. 59.

9   S. NYSTRÖM, *Beduinentum und Jahwismus*, Lund, C.W.K. Gleerup, 1946, p. 109; S. TALMON, *The "Desert Motif" in the Bible and in Qumran Literature*, in A. ALTMANN (ed.), *Biblical Motifs* (Studies and Texts, 3), Cambridge, MA, Harvard University Press, 1966, 31–64.

10 NYSTRÖM, *Beduinentum und Jahwismus*, p. 163; TALMON, *The "Desert Motif"*.

11 https://www.worldwildlife.org/ecoregions/pa1303.

12 M. HOPPAL, *Linguistic and Mental Models for Hungarian Folk Beliefs*, in A.-L. SIIKALA (ed.), *Myth and Mentality: Studies in Folklore and Popular Thought* (Studia Fennica Folkloristica / Suomalaisen Kirjallisuuden Seura, 8), Helsinki, Finnish Literature Society, 2002, 50–66, p. 54.

13 J. SZLAMOWICZ, *Food, Memory and the Blues*, in *Les mots du jazz*, Toulouse, Presses Universitaires du Midi, 2018, p. 123.
14 Cf. C.Y. TILLEY, *A Phenomenology of Landscape* (Explorations in Anthropology), Oxford, Berg, 1994, p. 24.
15 J. BORELLA, *The Crisis of Religious Symbolism & Symbolism and Reality*, trans. G.J. Champoux, Kettering, OH, Angelico, 2016, p. 43.
16 K. CRANE, *Wilderness Effects and Wild Affects in UK Nature/Travel Writing*, in I. HABERMANN—D. KELLER (eds.), *English Topographies in Literature and Culture* (Spatial Practices, 23), Leiden, E.J. Brill, 2016, 41–57, p. 47.
17 Defined with A.R. GRAY, *Psalm 18 in Words and Pictures* (Biblical Interpretation Series, 127), Leiden, Brill, 2014, p. 10, as an analogical word-picture, a strictly linguistic phenomenon; GRAY, *Psalm 18 in Words and Pictures*, p. 13. The desert image is far more 'alive' than any metaphor; HOPPAL, *Linguistic and Mental Models*, p. 56. Metaphors alone should not be used to reconstruct beliefs; L. HONKO, *Memorates and the Study of Folk Beliefs*, in *Journal of the Folklore Institute* 1 (1964) 5–19, p. 13.
18 C. GEERTZ, *"From the Native's Point of View": On the Art of Anthropological Understanding*, in *Bulletin of the American Academy of Arts and Sciences* 28 (1974) 26–45, p. 43.
19 GEERTZ, *Native's Point of View*, p. 43; as GRAY, *Psalm 18 in Words and Pictures*, p. 29 writes, 'Encyclopaedic knowledge must be considered when exploring a metaphor's meaning'.

II
Yahweh from the South

1 L. E. AXELSSON, *The Lord Rose up from Seir* (Coniectanea Biblica Old Testament Series, 15), Lund: Almqvist and Wiksell, 1987, p. 56.
2 R. D. MILLER II, *Oral Tradition in Ancient Israel* (Biblical Performance Criticism, 4), Eugene, Oregon: Cascade Books, 2011.
3 T. GUNNELL, *Nordic Folk Legends, Folk Traditions and Grave Mounds*, in *New Focus on Retrospective Methods:*

Notes to *The Corporal Desert*

Resuming Methodological Discussions: Case Studies from Northern Europe, ed. E. HEIDE and K. BEK-PEDERSEN (Folklore Fellows' Communications, 307), Helsinki: Suomalainen Tiedeakatemia, Academia Scientiarum Fennica, 2014, pp. 17–18.

4   That is, the mind does not see these as sequences of individual words. Such things are very common and not only as idioms; C. BUTLER, *Formulaic Language*, in *The Dynamics of Language Use: Functional and Contrastive Perspectives*, ed. C. BUTLER, M. DE LOS ÁNGELES GÓMEZ GONZÁLEZ, and S. M. DOVAL SUÁREZ (Pragmatics & Beyond, n.s. 140), Amsterdam: J. Benjamins, 2005, p. 223.

5   *Ibid.*, pp. 37–38, 44, 47.

6   *Ibid.*, p. 47.

III
The Corporal Desert

1   V. ANTTONEN, *Landscapes as Sacroscapes*, in S.W. NORDEIDE (ed.), *Sacred Sites and Holy Places* (Studies in the Early Middle Ages, 11) Turnhout, Brepols, 2013, 13–32, pp. 15–16; A.-L. SIIKALA, *Variation in the Incantation and Mythical Thinking*, in *Journal of Folklore Research* 23 (1986) 187–200, p. 190; A.-L. SIIKALA, *What Myths Tell about Past Finno-Ugric Modes of Thinking*, in A.-L. SIIKALA (ed.), *Myth and Mentality* (Studia Fennica Folkloristica / Suomalaisen Kirjallisuuden Seura, 8), Helsinki, Finnish Literature Society, 2002, 15–32, p. 17.

2   J. FRIEDENBERG—G. SILVERMAN, *Cognitive Science*, 2nd ed., Los Angeles, CA, Sage, 2012, pp. 2, 11. It is thus far more than just neuroscience.

3   B. SOM, *Toward a Cognitive Linguistics Understanding of Folk Narratives*, in *Lokaratna* 4 (2011) 54–63, p. 58; cf. BORELLA, *The Crisis of Religious Symbolism*, pp. 46, 385.

4   ANTTONEN, *Landscapes as Sacroscapes*, p. 19.

5   T.E. HALL—D.N. COLE, *Immediate Conscious Experience in Wilderness*, in D.N. COLE (ed.), *Wilderness Visitor Experiences* (USDA Forest Service Proceedings RMRS-P-

66), Missoula, MT: US Department of Agriculture, 2012, 37–49, p. 38.
6 J.A. VUCETICH – M.P. NELSON, *Distinguishing Experiential and Physical Conceptions of Wilderness*, in M.P. NELSON—J.B. CALLICOTT (eds.), *The Wilderness Debate Rages On: Continuing the Great New Wilderness Debate*, Athens, GA, University of Georgia Press, 2008, 611–631, p. 618.
7 W.P. KOPPEN—R. GEIGER, *Klima der Erde = Climate of the Earth*, Darmstadt, Justus Perthes, 1985.
8 T. LITTMANN—S.M. BERKOWICZ, *The Regional Climatic Setting*, in S.W. BRECKLE—A. YĀ'ÎR—M. VESTE (eds.), *Arid Dune Ecosystems: The Nizzana Sands in the Negev Desert* (Ecological Studies, 200), Berlin, Springer, 2008, 49–64, p. 54.
9 A. YĀ'ÎR, *The Ambiguous Impact of Climatic Change at the Desert Fringe*, in A.C. MILINGTON—K. PYE (eds.), *Environment Change in Drylands*, New York, NY, John Wiley & Sons, 1994, 199–227; Y. AVNI—N. PORAT—G. AVNI, *Pre-farming environment and OSL Chronology in the Negev Highlands, Israel*, in *Journal of Arid Environments* 86 (2012) 12–27.
10 S. P. MOSLUND, *The Presence of Place in Literature*, in R.T. TALLY (ed.), *Geocritical Explorations: Space, Place, and Mapping in Literary and Cultural Studies*, New York, NY, Palgrave Macmillan, 2011, 29–43, p. 30.
11 TILLEY, *A Phenomenology of Landscape*, p. 31.
12 MOSLUND, *Presence of Place in Literature*, pp. 31–35.
13 R. HAALAND—G. HAALAND, *Landscape*, in T. INSOLL (ed.), *The Oxford Handbook of the Archaeology of Ritual and Religion* (Oxford Handbooks), Oxford, Oxford University Press, 2011, 24–37, p. 25; E. CASSIRER, *Language and Myth*, New York, NY, Dover, [1925] 1953, pp. 9–11; B.C. LANE, *The Solace of Fierce Landscapes: Exploring Desert and Mountain Spirituality*, New York, NY, Oxford University Press, 1998, p. 16; already E. SAPIR, *Language and Environment*, in *American Anthropologist* 14 (1912) 226–242, p. 226.

Notes to *The Corporal Desert*

14 ANTTONEN, *Landscapes as Sacroscapes*, p. 13; DAVENPORT, *The Geography of the Imagination*, p. 4; J. KOURI, *Co-Composing a Village History in the Archipelago of South-western Finland*, in P. INGMAN (ed.), *The Relational Dynamics of Disenchantment and Sacralization* (The Study of Religion in a Global Context), Bristol, CT, Equinox Publishing, 2016, 231–250, p. 236; E. CRIST, *Against the Social Construction of Nature and Wilderness*, in M.P. NELSON—J.B. CALLICOTT (eds.), *The Wilderness Debate Rages On*, Athens, GA, University of Georgia Press, 2008, 500–525, pp. 507–508; BORELLA, *The Crisis of Religious Symbolism*, p. 389; BASSO, *Wisdom Sits in Places*, p. 108; D. LAWLOR, *Returning to Wirikuta*, in *European Journal of Ecopsychology* 4 (2013) 19–31, p. 22, with case examples from the Huichol Indians. Such 'extreme subjectivism' is already rejected in C. GEERTZ, *Thick description: Toward an interpretive theory of culture*, in *The Interpretation of Cultures*, New York, NY, Basic Books, 1973, 3–30.

15 J.V. WERTSCH, *Voices of Collective Remembering*, Cambridge, Cambridge University Press, 2002, p. 10.

16 MOSLUND, *Presence of Place in Literature*, pp. 35–37.

17 C. BRAWLEY, *Nature and the Numinous in Mythopoeic Fantasy Literature* (Critical Explorations in Science Fiction and Fantasy, 46), Jefferson, NC, McFarland, 2014, pp. 14, 16.

18 U. LINDEMANN, *Die Wüste: Terra incognita, Erlebnis, Symbol: eine Genealogie der abendländischen Wüstenvorstellungen in der Literatur von der Antike bis zur Gegenwart* (Beiträge zur neueren Literaturgeschichte, 3.175), Heidelberg, C. Winter, 2000, p. 13.

19 The voice of the desert's own inhabitants, which is missing in the Bible, does not see the desert as a unified 'thing' at all; P. HALEN—E. LECLERQ, *Désert et altérite*, in G. NAUROY—P. HALEN—A.-E. SPICA (eds.), *Le désert, un espace paradoxal* (Recherches en littérature et spiritualité, 2), Bern, Lang, 2003, 11–30, p. 17.

20 J. BAUDRILLARD, *America*, London, Verso, 2010, p. 6.

21 L. FELDT, *Wilderness and Hebrew Bible Religion*, in L. FELDT (ed.), *Wilderness in Mythology and Religion* (Religion and Society, 55), Boston, De Gruyter, 2012, 55–94, pp. 69, 82.
22 E. ABBEY, *Desert solitaire: A season in the wilderness*, London, Clark, 1992, pp. 241–242; K. S. WALTERS, *Soul Wilderness: A Desert Spirituality*, New York, NY, Paulist Press, 2001, p. 1. See A. MIQUEL, *Le désert dans la poésie arabe préislamique*, in *Les Mystiques du désert dans l'Islam, le judaïsme et le christianisme*, Gordes, France, Association des Amis de Sénanque, 1975, 73–88, pp. 78–81, on how these feature in pre-Islamic Arabic poetry.
23 G. GRESHAKE, *Die Wüste bestehen: Erlebnis und geistliche Erfahrung*, Kevelaer, Topos, 2004, p. 72; I. HOLM, *A Cultural Landscape beyond the Infield/Outfield Categories*, in *Norwegian Archaeological Review* 35 (2002) 67–80, p. 76. Howling wolves are also characteristic of Skaði's mountains in *Ynglinga saga* 8. Although wolves do not penetrate far into the desert, preferring to lurk in the reed beds of the desert fringes; D. L. HARRISON, *The Mammals of Arabia*, vol. 2, London, Ernest Benn, 1968, p. 202, they abound in the harsh mountains of the Saudi–Jordanian border; P.L. CUNNINGHAM—T. WRONSKI, *Arabian Wolf Distribution Update from Saudi Arabia*, in *Canid News* 13 (2010) no. 1, pp. 1, 3. Online: https://www.canids.org/canidnews/13/Arabian_wolf_in_Saudi_Arabia.pdf.
24 *Phenomenology of Perception*, cited in TILLEY, *A Phenomenology of Landscape*, p. 12.
25 W.T. BORRIE—J.W. ROGGENBUCK, *The Dynamic, Emergent, and Multi-Phasic Nature of On-Site Wilderness Experiences*, in *Journal of Leisure Research* 33 (2001) 202–228, pp. 205–207.
26 HALL—COLE, *Immediate Conscious Experience*, pp. 40–41, 44.
27 *Ibid.*, p. 41.
28 H.B. TRISTRAM, *The Natural History of the Bible*, 10th ed., London, SPCK, 1911, pp. 192–193.

Notes to *The Corporal Desert*

29 E. FIRMAGE, Zoology, in *Anchor Bible Dictionary*, Garden City, Doubleday, 1992.
30 D. SCOTT, *The Long-Eared Owl*, London, Hawk and Owl Trust, 1997, p. 31.
31 J.S. MARKS—D.L. EVANS—D.W. HOLT, *Long-eared Owl* (The Birds of North America, 33), Philadelphia, PA, The Academy of Natural Sciences, 1994, pp. 4–5; H. WIJNANDTS, *Ecological Energetics of the Long-Eared Owl (Asio Otus)*, in *Ardea* 13 (2002) 1–92, pp. 38–90.
32 MARKS—EVANS—HOLT, *Long-eared Owl*, p. 5.
33 *Ibid.*, p. 6.
34 TRISTRAM, *The Natural History of the Bible*, pp. 193–194.
35 D. NIEUWENHUYSE—J.-C. GÉNOT—D.H. JOHNSON, *The Little Owl: Conservation, Ecology and Behavior of Athene Noctua*, Cambridge, Cambridge University Press, 2008, p. 167.
36 *Ibid.*, p. 183; J.F. EISENBERG, *The Behavior Patterns of Desert Rodents*, in I. PRAKASH—P.K. GHOSH (eds.), *Rodents in Desert Environments* (Monographiae Biologicae, 28), The Hague, Junk, 1975, pp. 189–224.
37 NIEUWENHUYSE—GÉNOT—JOHNSON, *The Little Owl*, p. 225.
38 *Ibid.*, p. 230; the *qa'at* of Zeph 2,14 is the Pallid Scops Owl (*Otus brucei*); FIRMAGE, *Zoology*; H. SANGHA—D. MALIK, *Observations on wintering Pallid Scops Owl Otus brucei at Zainabad, Little Rann of Kachchh, Surendranagar district, Gujarat*, in *Indian Birds* 5 (2010) 176–177.
39 M.B. QUMSIYEH, *Mammals of the Holy Land*, Lubbock, TX, Texas Tech University Press, 1996, p. 176; HARRISON, *The Mammals of Arabia*, p. 279.
40 HARRISON, *The Mammals of Arabia*, p. 279.
41 QUMSIYEH, *Mammals of the Holy Land*, p. 177.
42 J. FILSER—R. PRASSE, *A Glance on the Fauna of Nizzana*, in S.W. BRECKLE—A. YĀʿĪR—M. VESTE (eds.), *Arid Dune Ecosystems* (Ecological Studies, 200), Berlin, Springer, 2008, 125–148, p. 128.
43 ABBEY, *Desert solitaire*, pp. 241–242.
44 K. TIELBORGER—R. PRASSE—H. LESCHNER, *The Flora of*

Notes to *The Corporal Desert*

the *Nizzana Research Site*, in S.W. BRECKLE—A. YĀʿĪR—M. VESTE (eds.), *Arid Dune Ecosystems* (Ecological Studies, 200), Berlin, Springer, 2008, 93–104, p. 101.

45 M.A. ZAHRAN—A.J. WILLIS, *The Vegetation of Egypt*, London, Chapman & Hall, 1992, p. 164; L.O. MANGER, *Survival on Meagre Resources: Hadendowa Pastoralism in the Red Sea Hills*, Uppsala, Nordiska Afrikainstitutet, 1996, pp. 46–47, 54.

46 A. DANIN, *Plants of Desert Dunes* (Adaptations of Desert Organisms), New York, NY, Springer, 1996, p. 85.

47 TIELBORGER—PRASSE—LESCHNER, *The Flora of the Nizzana*, p. 101.

48 DANIN, *Plants of Desert Dunes*, p. 134.

49 A. DE PURY, *L'image du désert dans l'Ancien Testament*, in Y. CHRISTE (ed.), *Le Désert: image et réalité* (Les Cahiers du Centre d'étude du Proche-Orient ancien, 3), Leuven, Peeters, 1989, 115–126, p. 118.

50 B. BRYSON, *A Walk in the Woods*, London, Corgi, 1998, p. 62.

51 M.E. PATTERSON ET AL., *An Hermeneutic Approach to Studying the Nature of Wilderness Experience*, in *Journal of Leisure Research* 30 (1998) 423–452, pp. 440–441.

52 ABBEY, *Desert solitaire*, p. 241.

53 K.-H. FLECKENSTEIN, *Botschaft der Wüste*, Innsbruck, Tyrolia-Verlag, 2016, p. 95; GRESHAKE, *Die Wüste bestehen*, p. 11; N.J. COETZEE, *Wild God in the Wilderness: Why does Yahweh choose to appear in the Wilderness in the Book of Exodus?*, PhD Diss., Birmingham, University of Birmingham, 2016, p. 319.

54 J.S. JABBŪR, *The Bedouins and the Desert: Aspects of Nomadic Life in the Arab East* (SUNY Series in Near Eastern Studies), Albany, NY, State University of New York Press, 1995, pp. 44–46; DANIN, *Plants of Desert Dunes*, p. 88; GRESHAKE, *Die Wüste bestehen*, p. 65; M.T. AHMED, ed., *Ecosystems and Human Well-Being: El Maghara, Northern Sinai, Egypt*, Nairobi, UNEP, 2010, pp. 78–79.

55 MANGER, *Survival on Meagre Resources*, p. 42.

56 ZAHRAN—WILLIS, *The Vegetation of Egypt*, pp. 65, 206.

Notes to *Participant Observation*

57 C.W. FAGG—A. GREAVES—K. LANGDON, *Acacia Tortilis: 1925–1988* (Annotated Bibliography / CAB F41), Oxford, CAB International, 1990, p. 36.
58 GRESHAKE, *Die Wüste bestehen*, pp. 65–66.
59 TRISTRAM, *The Natural History of the Bible*, p. 464.
60 FILSER—PRASSE, *A Glance on the Fauna*, p. 125.
61 JABBŪR, *The Bedouins*, p. 48.
62 GRESHAKE, *Eine Landschaft*, p. 20, italics original. GRESHAKE, *Spiritualität der Wüste*, pp. 49–52.

IV
Participant Observation

1 M. ALDENDERFER, *Envisioning a pragmatic approach to the archaeology of religion*, in Y.M. ROWAN (ed.), *Beyond belief: the archaeology of religion and ritual* (Archaeological Papers of the American Anthropological Association, 21), Hoboken, NJ, American Anthropological Association, 2012, 23–36, p. 31.
2 TILLEY, *A Phenomenology of Landscape*, p. 11.
3 M. JOHNSON, *Ideas of Landscape*, Oxford, Blackwell, 2007, pp. 26, 33.
4 TILLEY, *A Phenomenology of Landscape*, p. 15.
5 P. BOURDIEU, *Outline of a Theory of Practice*, 25th ed. (Cambridge Studies in Social and Cultural Anthropology, 16), Cambridge, Cambridge University Press, [1972] 2010, p. 19.
6 *Ibid.*, p. 115.
7 KOURI, *Co-Composing a Village History*, pp. 232, 237–238; LANE, *The Solace of Fierce Landscapes*, p. 19; BASSO, *Wisdom sits in places*, pp. 68–69. This is the mainstay of ethnography since B. MALINOWSKI, *Argonauts of the Western Pacific*, London, Routledge & Kegan Paul, 1922; B. MALINOWSKI, *Method and Scope of Anthropological Fieldwork*, in A.C.G.M. ROBBEN—J.A. SLUKA (eds.), *Ethnographic fieldwork: an anthropological reader*, 2nd ed. (Blackwell Anthologies in Social and Cultural Anthropology), Malden, MA, Wiley-Blackwell, [1922] 2012, 69–81, pp. 71–73; M.S. SCHWARTZ—C.G. SCHWARTZ,

Notes to *Participant Observation*

Problems in Participant Observation, in *American Journal of Sociology* 60 (1955) 343–353, p. 349, although Boas certainly introduced the concept; E.E. EVANS-PRITCHARD, *Fieldwork and the Empirical Tradition*, in *Fieldwork*, vol. 1 (Sage Benchmarks in Social Research Methods), Thousand Oaks, CA, Sage, [1951] 2005, 103–115, pp. 107–109. For a critical assessment of Malinowski's practice, see G.W. STOCKING JR., *The Ethnographer's Magic—Fieldwork in British Anthropology from Tylor to Malinowski*, in *Fieldwork*, vol. 1 (Sage Benchmarks in Social Research Methods), Thousand Oaks, CA, Sage, 2005, 218–263, pp. 248–256.

8   MALINOWSKI, *Method and Scope*, p. 79.
9   ABBEY, *Desert solitaire*, p. 11.
10 GRESHAKE, *Eine Landschaft*, p. 19.
11 A. HUXLEY, *The Desert*, in *Adonis and the Alphabet*, London, Chatto & Windus, 1956, p. 77.
12 BAUDRILLARD, *America*, p. 6.
13 J.W. KRUTCH, *The Voice of the Desert: A Naturalist's Interpretation*, New York, NY, William Sloane, 1966, p. 13.
14 *Ibid.*
15 KRUTCH, *The Voice of the* Desert, p. 14.
16 *Ibid.*, p. 17.
17 *Ibid.*, p. 214.
18 SCHWARTZ AND SCHWARTZ, 'Problems in Participant Observation', p. 344. On the inescapability of such 'investment,' see Geertz, 'Native's Point of View', p. 27, and already MALINOWSKI, 'Method and Scope', p. 77; on our inability to ever truly 'participate,' see E. E. EVANS-PRITCHARD, 'Some reminiscences and reflections on fieldwork (Appendix IV)', in *Witchcraft, Oracles, and Magic among the Azande*, ed. E. E. Evans-Pritchard and E. Gillies; Oxford: Clarendon, 1976, p. 3.
19 T. INSOLL, *Archaeology, Ritual, Religion*, New York: Routledge, 2004, pp. 88, 93.
20 INSOLL, *Archaeology, Ritual, Religion*, pp. 93, 95.
21 GEERTZ, 'Native's Point of View', p. 29; also Basso, *Wisdom Sits in Places*, p. 110.

Notes to *Participant Observation*

22. GEERTZ, 'Native's Point of View', p. 29.
23. I. HABERMANN, 'Running Rings Round London: Psychogeography in Iain Sinclair's London Orbital', in *English Topographies in Literature and Culture*, ed. I. Habermann and D. Keller (Spatial Practices 23) Leiden: Brill, 2016, p. 61; W. SELF, *Psychogeography: Disentangling the Modern Conundrum of Psyche and Place*, New York: Bloomsbury, 2007, p. 11.
24. S. OVERALL, "The Walking Dead: Or Why Psychogeography Matters" (paper presented at the Re-enchanting the Academy, Canterbury Christ Church University, 2015) 1, accessed 4 January 2017, https://www.canterbury.ac.uk/education/conferences-events/re-enchanting-the-academy/assets/sonia-overall.pdf; G. DEBORD, "Theory of the Dérive," *Les Lèvres nues*, November 1959 1, www.cddc.vt.edu/sionline/si/theory.html; D. WOOD, "Lynch Debord: About Two Psychogeographies," *Cartographica: The International Journal for Geographic Information and Geovisualization* 45 (2010) 186.
25. G. DEBORD, 'Introduction to a Critique of Urban Geography', *Les Lèvres Nues*, 1955 1, Online: http://library.nothingness.org/articles/SI/en/display/2.
26. HABERMANN, 'Running Rings', 63; Wood, 'Lynch Debord', 195; DEBORD, 'Introduction to a Critique of Urban Geography', 3–4.
27. OVERALL, 'Walking Dead', 2.
28. OVERALL, 'Walking Dead', 4.
29. OVERALL, 'Walking Dead', 8.
30. OVERALL, 'Walking Dead', 5.
31. OVERALL, 'Walking Dead', 7–8.
32. I. BROOK, 'Goethean Science as a Way to Read Landscape', *Landscape Research* 23 1 (1998) 60; N. DUNCAN and J. DUNCAN, 'Doing Landscape Interpretation', in *The Sage Handbook of Qualitative Geography*, ed. D. DELYSER et al.; Los Angeles: Sage, 2010, p. 229.
33. P. GEMEINBOECK, 'Impossible Geographies', in *Intensive Science* (Exhibition catalogue) Paris: Sony CSL, 2006, p. 1.

Notes to *Participant Observation*

34 OVERALL, 'Walking Dead', 8.
35 GEMEINBOECK, 'Impossible Geographies', 2; DUNCAN and DUNCAN, 'Doing Landscape Interpretation', 243.
36 WOOD, 'Lynch Debord', 186, 188.
37 WOOD, 'Lynch Debord', 190.
38 WOOD, 'Lynch Debord', 191.
39 C. HOLDREGE, 'Doing Goethean Science', *Janus Head* 8 1 (2005) 30.
40 BROOK, 'Goethean Science', 52.
41 HOLDREGE, 'Doing Goethean Science', 31.
42 HOLDREGE, 'Doing Goethean Science', 31.
43 DUNCAN AND DUNCAN, 'Doing Landscape Interpretation', 242.
44 OVERALL, 'Walking Dead', 3.
45 OVERALL, 'Walking Dead', 3.
46 DEBORD, 'Theory of the Dérive', 1; WOOD, 'Lynch Debord', 194; GEMEINBOECK, 'Impossible Geographies', 1.
47 DEBORD, 'Theory of the Dérive', p. 2; WOOD, 'Lynch Debord', p. 187.
48 OVERALL, 'Walking Dead', p. 2.
49 OVERALL, 'Walking Dead', p. 9.
50 OVERALL, 'Walking Dead', p. 9.
51 OVERALL, 'Walking Dead', p. 9; BROOK, 'Goethean Science', p. 54.
52 DEBORD, 'Theory of the Dérive', p. 1.
53 DEBORD, 'Introduction to a Critique of Urban Geography', p. 3; BROOK, 'Goethean Science', p. 65.
54 DEBORD, 'Theory of the Dérive', p. 1.
55 BROOK, 'Goethean Science', p. 53.
56 HOLDREGE, 'Doing Goethean Science', p. 48.
57 OVERALL, 'Walking Dead', p. 9; BROOK, 'Goethean Science', p. 53; SCHWARTZ AND SCHWARTZ, 'Problems in Participant Observation', p. 345.
58 BROOK, 'Goethean Science', p. 54.
59 OVERALL, 'Walking Dead', p. 9.
60 HOLDREGE, 'Doing Goethean Science', p. 35.

Notes to *Desert Wind*

61 HOLDREGE, 'Doing Goethean Science', p. 49; BROOK, 'Goethean Science', p. 53.
62 OVERALL, 'Walking Dead', p. 9; BROOK, 'Goethean Science', p. 58. On emotion in wilderness experience, see BORRIE and ROGGENBUCK, 'Dynamic, Emergent, and Multi-Phasic Nature', p. 221.
63 HOLDREGE, 'Doing Goethean Science', p. 50; BROOK, 'Goethean Science', p. 52; SCHWARTZ AND SCHWARTZ, 'Problems in Participant Observation', p. 345.
64 L. BRODKEY, 'Writing Ethnographic Narratives', *Written Communication* 4 (1987) 26, 32.
65 C. GEERTZ, 'Being There (1988)', in *Fieldwork*, ed. C. Pole; vol. 4 (Sage Benchmarks in Social Research Methods) Thousand Oaks: Sage, 2005, p. 136.
66 In addition, there is a strong resistance, a psychogeographical boundary, at the Nahal Havarim.
67 Cf. GRESHAKE, 'Eine Landschaft', p. 19.
68 GEERTZ, 'Native's Point of View', p. 30.

V
Desert Wind

1 FLECKENSTEIN, *Botschaft der Wüste*, p. 89; WALTERS, *Soul Wilderness*, p. 85 speaks of 'Holy Sirocco.'
2 FLECKENSTEIN, *Botschaft der Wüste*, p. 99; P. BRYDONE— W. BECKFORD—J.F. JUNIUS, *P. Brydone's Reise durch Sicilien und Malta, in Briefen an William Beckford. Esq. zu Somerly in Suffolk: nebst einer Charte von Sicilien und Malta*, Leipzig, Bey Johann Friedrich Junius, 1777, p. 345.
3 C.C. HELD, *Middle East Patterns: Places, Peoples, and Politics*, 3rd ed., Boulder, CO, Westview, 2000, p. 63.
4 T. SIVALL, *Sirocco in the Levant*, in *Geografiska Annaler* 39 (1957) 114–142, p. 116.
5 BRYDONE—BECKFORD—JUNIUS, *P. Brydone's Reise durch Sicilien und Malta*, p. 345; SIVALL, *Sirocco in the Levant*, p. 121; J. GREGOIRE, *Du Khamsin et des ses effets*, in *Mémoires ou travaux originaux présentés et lus à l'Institut égyptien* 1 (1862) 369–382, p. 369.

Notes to *The Textual Desert*

6 SIVALL, *Sirocco in the Levant*, pp. 117–118, 122; TRISTRAM, *The Natural History of the Bible*, p. 33.
7 GREGOIRE, *Du Khamsin*, p. 370.
8 SIVALL, *Sirocco in the Levant*, p. 122; GREGOIRE, *Du Khamsin*, pp. 369, 372.
9 HELD, *Middle East patterns*, p. 63; GREGOIRE, *Du Khamsin*, p. 370.
10 JABBŪR, *The Bedouins*, p. 50.
11 T.E. LAWRENCE, *Seven Pillars of Wisdom*, London, Jonathan Cape, 1935, p. 205.
12 SIVALL, *Sirocco in the Levant*, p. 116.
13 C.B. MICHAELIS, *Hagiographos*, Halle, Germany, Orphanotrophei, 1720, vol. 2. at Job 37,17; GREGOIRE, *Du Khamsin*, p. 370.
14 LAWRENCE, *Seven Pillars of Wisdom*, p. 205.
15 GREGOIRE, *Du Khamsin*, pp. 370, 376; BRYDONE—BECKFORD—JUNIUS, *P. Brydone's Reise durch Sicilien und Malta*, p. 345.
16 JABBŪR, *The Bedouins*, pp. 50–51.
17 LAWRENCE, *Seven Pillars of Wisdom*, p. 206.

VI
The Textual Desert

1 BRAWLEY, *Nature and the Numinous*, p. 13.
2 *Ibid.*; Y. TUAN, *Space and Place: The Perspective of Experience*, Minneapolis, MN, University of Minnesota Press, 1977, p. 162.
3 BRAWLEY, *Nature and the Numinous*, p. 14.
4 M.H. KELLY—F.C. KEIL, *Metaphor Comprehension and Knowledge of Semantic Domains*, in P. HANKS—R. GIORA (eds.), *Metaphor and figurative language* (Critical Concepts in Linguistics, 3), Abingdon, United Kingdom, Routledge, 2012, 511–528, pp. 512, 525. Based on experimental studies.
5 ANTTONEN, *Landscapes as Sacroscapes*, p. 23; M. TAYLOR, *Swimming in the flax field, verða at gjalti, and related matters*, in J. LINDOW—G. CLARK (eds.), *Frederic Amory in*

Notes to *The Textual Desert*

Memoriam: Old Norse-Icelandic Studies, Berkeley, CA, North Pinehurst Press, 2015, 91–134, p. 91.

6   TAYLOR, *Swimming in the Flax Field*, pp. 94, 103.
7   N. WYATT, *The Vocabulary and Neurology of Orientation*, in N. WYATT—W.G.E. WATSON—LLOYD (eds.), *Ugarit, Religion and Culture*, Münster, Ugarit-Verlag, 1996, 351–380, p. 361.
8   M.P. O'CONNOR, *Cardinal-Direction Terms in Biblical Hebrew*, in A.S. KAYE (ed.), *Semitic Studies*, 2 vols., Wiesbaden, Harrassowitz, 1991, pp. 2:1143, 1145.
9   WYATT, *Vocabulary and Neurology*, p. 362.
10 WYATT, *Vocabulary and Neurology*, p. 363.
11 *Ibid.*, pp. 356, 363.
12 TILLEY, *A Phenomenology of Landscape*, p. 14.
13 WYATT, *Vocabulary and Neurology*, p. 364.
14 W.D. HOPKINS, *Laterality in Maternal Cradling and Infant Positional Biases: Implications for the Development and Evolution of Hand Preferences in Nonhuman Primates*, in *International Journal of Primatology* 25 (2004) 1243–1265; J. VAUCLAIR—C. SCOLA, *Infant-holding biases in mothers and affective symptoms during pregnancy and after delivery*, in *Infant and Child Development* 18 (2009) 106–121.
15 WYATT, *Vocabulary and Neurology*, pp. 364–365.
16 *Ibid.*, p. 366.
17 *Ibid.*, p. 373.
18 WYATT, *Vocabulary and Neurology*, p. 370.
19 J. MONTGOMERY, *Arabia and the Bible,* New York, NY, Ktav, [1934] 1969, p. 170.
20 WALTERS, *Soul Wilderness*, p. 9.
21 O'CONNOR, *Cardinal-Direction Terms*, p. 2:1146, where he dismisses Childs's proposal.
22 M. COMINS, *A Wild Faith: Jewish Ways into Wilderness, Wilderness Ways into Judaism*, Woodstock, VT, Jewish Lights Publishing, 2007, p. 138.
23 COETZEE, *Wild God in the Wilderness*, p. 335.
24 J. BARR, *Migraš in the Old Testament*, in *Journal of Semitic Studies* 29 (1984) 15–31, pp. 24–25, first argued by

Notes to *The Textual Desert*

O. PROCKSCH in the λεγω entry of *Theological Dictionary of the New Testament*; A.C. THISELTON, *The Supposed Power of Words in the Biblical Writings*, in *Journal of Theological Studies* 25 (1974) 283–299, p. 289; P.N. TARAZI, *The Rise of Scripture*, St. Paul, MN, Orthodox Center for the Advancement of Biblical Studies, 2017, pp. 92–94, argues it is the same root as *dabar*, "word," citing as evidence Song 4,3, where *midbarim* clearly means "words" (of the "mouth")—as the Septuagint knows—but in the context of terms pertaining to oasis life; also Isa 5,17 and Mic 2,12, where *dober* clearly means "wilderness". But he also notes Pss 18,48; 47,4, where the hiphil *hidbir* means "drive back", allowing "back" as the base meaning.

25 COETZEE, *Wild God in the Wilderness*, p. 28.
26 The analysis of this word in FELDT, *Wilderness and Hebrew Bible Religion*, p. 65, is entirely without reference to biblical passages.
27 WALTERS, *Soul Wilderness*, p. 13; DE PURY, *L'image du desert*, p. 118.
28 COETZEE, *Wild God in the Wilderness*, pp. 329–330; TARAZI, *The Rise of Scripture*, p. 86 derives 'Zion' from this same root.
29 COETZEE, *Wild God in the Wilderness*, p. 327; DE PURY, *L'image du desert*, p. 117.
30 BAUDRILLARD, *America*, p. 6.
31 COETZEE, *Wild God in the Wilderness*, pp. 326–327.
32 BASSO, *Wisdom sits in places*, p. 130.
33 HYMES, *Foundations in Sociolinguistics*, p. 126.
34 D. MAINGUENEAU, *L'Énonciation en linguistique française* (Les fondamentaux cycle 1.29), Paris, Hachette, 1996, p. 9; HYMES, *Foundations in Sociolinguistics*, pp. 132–133.
35 MAINGUENEAU, *L'Énonciation*, p. 9.
36 E. BENVENISTE, *L'appareil formel de l'énonciation*, in *Langages* 5.17 (1970) 12–18, p. 13.
37 MAINGUENEAU, *L'Énonciation*, pp. 9–10; BENVENISTE, *L'appareil formel de l'énonciation*, pp. 12, 15; cf. R. GUÉNON, *Fundamental Symbols*, Oxford, Alden, 1962, p. 29; HYMES, *Foundations in Sociolinguistics*, p. 130.

Notes to *The Textual Desert*

38 BENVENISTE, *L'appareil formel de l'énonciation*, pp. 13–14; D. MAINGUENEAU, *La situation d'énonciation entre langue et discours*, in *Dix ans de S.D.U.*, Craiova, Romania, Editura Universitaria Craiova, 2004, 197–210, p. 197. Similar is the ca. 5th cent. AD Hindu language theory of Audumbarāyaṇa, Bhartṛhari, and Vārtākṣa that viewed the sentence as where meaning is normally attached, words being an artificial creation of lexicographers and those trying to teach children language; J. BROUGH, *Audumbarāyaṇa's Theory of Language*, in *Bulletin of the School of Oriental and Asian Studies* 14 (1952) 73–77, pp. 75–76; see Vākyapadīya, 2.345–349.

39 See HYMES, *Foundations in Sociolinguistics*, p. 127, on errors of Malinowski, Sapir, and others who abstracted from cultural context.

40 Cf. MAINGUENEAU, *La situation d'énonciation*, pp. 199–205.

41 MAINGUENEAU, *L'Énonciation*, p. 14.

42 *Ibid.*

43 R.B. LEAL, *Wilderness in the Bible: Toward a theology of wilderness* (Studies in Biblical Literature, 72), New York, NY, P. Lang, 2004, ignores the poetic passages Deut 33, etc., entirely in his monograph, considering the overriding viewpoint of the Hebrew Bible to be "abhorrence of wilderness."; also R.B. LEAL, *Negativity toward Wilderness in the Biblical Record*, in *Ecotheology* 10 (2005) 364–381.

44 J. PEDERSEN, *Israel, Its Life and Culture*, London, Oxford University Press, 1926, pp. 456–468; GRESHAKE, *Spiritualität der Wüste*, pp. 46–48; V. ZARINI, *Aspects et paradoxes du désert dans une épopée latine de l'Afrique chrétienne du VIe siècle*, in G. NAUROY – P. HALEN—A.-E. SPICA (eds.), *Le désert, un espace paradoxal: actes du colloque de l'Université de Metz, 13–15 septembre 2001* (Recherches en littérature et spiritualité, 2), Bern, Lang, 2003, 143–157, p. 153.

45 GRESHAKE, *Die Wüste bestehen*, p. 26; T. STAUBLI, *Das Image der Nomaden im alten Israel und in der Ikonographie seiner sesshaften Nachbarn* (Orbis Biblicus et Orientalis,

107), Freiburg, Switzerland, Universitätsverlag, 1991, p. 262; NYSTRÖM, *Beduinentum und Jahwismus*, p. 122.

46 A. HALDAR, *The Notion of the Desert in Sumero-Accadian and West-Semitic Religions*, in *Uppsala universitets årsskrift* 3 (1950) 11–70, p. 13; L. FELDT, *Religion, Nature, and Ambiguous Space in Ancient Mesopotamia: The Mountain Wilderness in Old Babylonian Religious Narratives*, in *Numen* 63 (2016) 347–382, p. 357.

47 FELDT, *Religion, Nature, and Ambiguous Space*, pp. 348–349.

48 *Ibid.*, pp. 363–371.

49 FELDT, *Religion, Nature, and Ambiguous Space*, p. 373.

50 S. LACKENBACHER, *L'image du désert d'après les textes littéraires assyro-babyloniens*, in Y. CHRISTE (ed.), *Le Désert: image et réalité* (Les Cahiers du CEPOA, 3), Leuven, Peeters, 1989, 57–65, pp. 62, 65.

51 *CAD* 10.1.12.

52 *CAD* 6.251.

53 W.W. LEE, *The Concept of the Wilderness in the Pentateuch*, in K.E. POMYKALA (ed.), *Israel in the wilderness: interpretations of the biblical narratives in Jewish and Christian traditions* (Themes in Biblical Narrative, 10), Leiden, Brill, 2008, 1–16, pp. 5–6, 15–16; FELDT, *Wilderness and Hebrew Bible Religion*, p. 70.

54 T.L. BURDEN, *The Kerygma of the Wilderness Traditions in the Hebrew Bible* (American University Studies Theology and Religion, 7.163), New York, NY, Peter Lang, 1994.

55 WALTERS, *Soul Wilderness*, pp. 13–14; GRESHAKE, *Die Wüste bestehen*, pp. 28–29; L. WALL, *Finding Identity in the Wilderness*, in B. MCGINN (ed.), *Meister Eckhart and the Beguine Mystics*, New York, NY, Continuum, 1994, 66–77, pp. 67–68, considers these to be a later development, but only by seeing the 'creeds' of Deuteronomy 6 and 26 as pre-8th cent. understandings of the wilderness. On the problems of the dating of these creeds, see R.D. MILLER II, *Covenant and grace in the Old Testament* (Perspectives on Hebrew Scriptures and its Contexts, 16), Piscataway, NJ, Gorgias, 2012. DE PURY, *L'image du desert*, p. 125, and TALMON, *The*

Notes to *The Folkloric Desert*

"*Desert Motif*", see these 'closeness' passages as of minor importance and as depending on an understanding of the wilderness as hell.
56 FELDT, *Wilderness and Hebrew Bible Religion*, p. 71.
57 G.H. WILLIAMS, *Wilderness and Paradise in Christian Thought* (Menno Simons Lectures), New York, NY, Harper & Brothers, 1962, pp. 15–16.
58 MICHAELIS, *Hagiographos*, p. 2.630; GRESHAKE, *Die Wüste bestehen*, p. 26.
59 GRESHAKE, *Spiritualität der Wüste*, p. 24–27.
60 GRESHAKE, *Die Wüste bestehen*, p. 32; COETZEE, *Wild God in the Wilderness*, p. 38.
61 GRESHAKE, *Spiritualität der Wüste*, p. 30.

VII
The Folkloric Desert
1 GRESHAKE, *Die Wüste bestehen*, p. 99.
2 E. GOODWYN, *Recurrent Motifs as Resonant Attractor States in the Narrative Field*, in *Journal of Analytic Psychology* 58 (2013) 387–408, p. 387.
3 GOODWYN, *Recurrent Motifs*, pp. 387–388. The desert would fall under what Jung called Architectural and Natural Archetypes; A.N. CARROLL, *Religious Symbolism, Jungian Archetypal Theory, and an Encounter with Evil* (PhD diss.), Washington, DC, Catholic University of America, 2012, p. 149.
4 M.A. MATTOON, *Jung and the Human Psyche: An Understandable Introduction*, London, Routledge, 2005, p. 35.
5 C.G. JUNG, *Approaching the unconscious*, in C.G. JUNG—M.-L. VON FRANZ (eds.), *Man and His Symbols*, Garden City, NJ, Doubleday, 1964, 18–103, p. 67; MATTOON, *Jung and the Human Psyche*, p. 36; M.-L. VON FRANZ, *Archetypal Dimensions of the Psyche*, Boston, MA, Shambhala, 1997, p. 6.
6 M. LINGS, *Symbol & Archetype: A Study of the Meaning of Existence* (Louisville, KY, Fons Vitae, 2006, pp. 1–2,

Notes to *The Folkloric Desert*

capitalization original; LINGS, *Symbol & Archetype*, p. 16, explicitly distances himself from Jungian psychology, but appears to be of much the same mind as Jung himself. The opposition to Jung from such Perennial Philosophers comes from an insistence that an archetype cannot both have a spiritual foundation and also be an inherited disposition; either "Archetypes are the source of being and knowledge" or they are "unconscious dispositions . . . to imagin[ation]"; T. BURCKHARDT, *Mirror of the Intellect: Essays on Traditional Science & Sacred Art* (SUNY Series in Islam), Albany, NY, State University of New York Press, 1987, pp. 59–60.

7 JUNG, *Approaching the Unconscious*, p. 67.
8 LINGS, *Symbol & Archetype*, p. 4.
9 GOODWYN, *Recurrent Motifs*, pp. 388–389; cf. JUNG, *Approaching the Unconscious*, p. 69.
10 LACKENBACHER, *Les textes littéraires assyro-babyloniens*, p. 64.
11 GOODWYN, *Recurrent Motifs*, p. 390; M. STEIN, *Jung's Map of the Soul: An Introduction*, Chicago, IL, Open Court, 1998, p. 100.
12 GOODWYN, *Recurrent Motifs*, p. 391; B. TOELKEN, *The Dynamics of Folklore*, Rev. ed., Logan, UT, Utah State University Press, 1996, pp. 413–415; FRANZ, *Archetypal Dimensions of the Psyche*, p. 112; but see BEREZKIN, *Folklore and Mythology Catalogue*, p. 62 on the uselessness of these older indices.
13 DUNCAN—DUNCAN, *Doing Landscape Interpretation*, p. 243.
14 GOODWYN, *Recurrent Motifs*, p. 394.
15 *Ibid.*
16 *Ibid.*, pp. 396–398; GOODWYN, *The Neurobiology of the Gods*, New York: Routledge, 2012, p. 32.
17 GOODWYN, *Recurrent Motifs*, p. 398.
18 *Ibid.*, p. 400.
19 N. QUINN, *The Cultural Basis of Metaphor* (1991), in P. HANKS—R. GIORA (eds.), *Metaphor and Figurative*

Notes to *The Folkloric Desert*

Language (Critical Concepts in Linguistics, 3), Abingdon, United Kingdom, Routledge, 2012, 133–163, pp. 139–141, 144, 146.
20 SOM, *Toward a Cognitive Linguistics Understanding*, p. 62.
21 REID, *Essays on the Intellectual Powers*, p. 479.
22 *Ibid.*, p. 483.
23 B. MCGINN, *Ocean and Desert as Symbols of Mystical Absorption in the Christian Tradition*, in *JR* 74 (1994) 155–181; GRESHAKE, *Die Wüste bestehen*, p. 15; KRUTCH, *Voice of the Desert*, p. 220.
An Akkadian hymn implores Shamash's help for those at sea or in the desert; LACKENBACHER, *Les textes littéraires assyro-babyloniens*, p. 70. The sea was off limits as a divine metaphor for Israel, however, since Yamm or the Sea was the primeval foe of God.
24 C.O. WORMAN, *Trooping fairies, trolls, and talking tigers: the influence of traditional wilderness archetypes on current land use patterns*, in *Biodiversity and Conservation* 19 (2010) 3171–3193, pp. 3176–3179.
25 WORMAN, *Trooping fairies*, pp. 3179, 3182. The place of the wilderness in Irish folklore is filled by locations around barrow tombs; WORMAN, *Trooping fairies*, p. 3186.
26 WORMAN, *Trooping fairies*, pp. 3183–3184; LANE, *The Solace of Fierce Landscapes*, p. 41.
27 WORMAN, *Trooping fairies*, p. 3190.
28 *Ibid.*
29 R. LEBRUN, *Les Hittites et le désert*, in Y. CHRISTE (ed.), *Le Désert: image et réalité* (Les Cahiers du CEPOA, 3), Leuven, Peeters, 1989, 81–88, p. 85.
30 A. ROCCATI, *La conception rituelle du désert chez les anciens Égyptiens*, in Y. CHRISTE (ed.), *Le Désert: image et réalité* (Les Cahiers du CEPOA, 3), Leuven, Peeters, 1989, 127–130, pp. 127–128.
31 *Ibid.*, p. 129.
32 J.N. BREMMER, *Greek Demons of the Wilderness*, in L. FELDT (ed.), *Wilderness in Mythology and Religion* (Religion and Society, 55), Boston, MA, De Gruyter, 2012, 25–54, p. 25.

For a thorough discussion of mountain imagery in Homer, see E. WAGNER, *Mountain-Man: Hebrew Bible Narrative Imagery in Light of Personified Mountains*, Diss., Washington, DC, The Catholic University of America, 2020.

33 BREMMER, *Greek Demons*, p. 27.
34 *Ibid.*
35 J.J.H. ROSSETTI, *Darkness in the Desert: Tradition and Transgression in Ibrāhīm al-Kūnī's Ushb al-Layl*, in *Journal of Arabic Literature* 42 (2011) 49–66, p. 61.
36 T. HOFFMANN, *Notes on Qur'anic Wisdom*, in L. FELDT (ed.), *Wilderness in Mythology and Religion* (Religion and Society, 55), Boston, MA, De Gruyter, 2012, 157–182, p. 161.
37 *Ibid.*, pp. 170, 174–175.
38 A. BIRRELL, ed., *The Classic of Mountains and Seas*, London, Penguin Putnam, 1999, pp. 159–188.
39 *Ibid.*, p. 174.
40 *Ibid.*, p. 24.
41 C. MALAMOUD, *Village et foret dans l'idéologie de l'Inde brahmanique*, in *European Journal of Sociology* 17 (1976) 3–20, p. 4; F. ZIMMERMANN, *The Jungle and the Aroma of Meats* (Comparative Studies of Health Systems and Medical Care, 20), Berkeley, CA, University of California Press, 1987, pp. 1–95 and passim, note esp. p. 71.
42 ZIMMERMANN, *The Jungle and the Aroma of Meats*, p. 39.
43 VIṢṆUŚARMAN, *The Five Discourses on Worldly Wisdom*, trans. P. Olivelle, New York, NY, New York University Press, 2006, pp. 61, 105.
44 MALAMOUD, *Village et foret*, p. 5.
45 *Ibid.*, p. 14.
46 ZIMMERMANN, *The Jungle and the Aroma of Meats*, p. 37; MALAMOUD, *Village et foret*, pp. 11–12; M.C.Q. FIBIGER, *Wilderness as Necessary Feature in Hindu Religion*, in L. FELDT (ed.), *Wilderness in Mythology and Religion* (Religion and Society, 55), Boston, MA, De Gruyter, 2012, 131–156, p. 133.
47 C. LARRINGTON, trans., *The Poetic Edda* (Oxford World's Classics), Oxford, Oxford University Press, 2008, p. 23.

Notes to *The Folkloric Desert*

48 S. STURLUSON, *Edda* (Everyman Classics, 499), trans. A. FAULKES, London, Dent, 1987, pp. 21, 74, 80–81; HOLM, *A Cultural Landscape*, p. 68. On trolls, see A. JAKOBSSON, *The Trollish Acts of Thorgrimr the Witch*, Saga-Book, 39–66, pp. 42–50, although his reliance on Snorra Sturluson and the Grimms is problematic; see T. GUNNELL, *How Elvish Were the Alfar?*, in A. WAWN (ed.), *Constructing Nations, Reconstructing Myth* (Making the Middle Ages, 9), Turnhout, Brepols, 2007, 111–130, pp. 113–115.
49 GUNNELL, *How Elvish Were the Alfar?*, p. 117.
50 *Ibid.*
51 *Ibid.*, p. 123.
52 *Ibid.*, pp. 118–120.
53 HOLM, *A Cultural Landscape*, p. 70.
54 TUAN, *Space and Place*, p. 86; TRISTRAM, *The Natural History of the Bible*, p. 14; HOLM, *A Cultural Landscape*, p. 71. Nevertheless, there was a physical boundary, sometimes marked by menhirs; HOLM, *A Cultural Landscape*, p. 73.
55 TUAN, *Space and Place*, p. 88.
56 G.W. BURNETT—R. JOULIE-KUTTNER—K.W. KANG'ETHE, *A Willing Benefactor: An Essay on Wilderness in Nilotic and Bantu Culture*, in M.P. NELSON—J.B. CALLICOTT (eds.), *The Wilderness Debate Rages on: Continuing the Great New Wilderness Debate*, Athens, GA, University of Georgia Press, 2008, 282–299, p. 293.
57 *Ibid.*, p. 285.
58 G.W. BURNETT—K.W. KANG'ETHE, *Wilderness and the Bantu Mind*, in *Environmental Ethics* 16 (1994) 145–160, pp. 151–152.
59 *Ibid.*, p. 153.
60 J.M. KARI ET AL., eds., *Shem Pete's Alaska: The Territory of the Upper Cook Inlet Dena'ina*, 2nd ed., Fairbanks, AK, University of Alaska Press, 2003, p. 149.
61 *Ibid.*, pp. 142, 163.
62 S. OLDEN, *Shoshone Folk Lore*, Milwaukee, WI, Morehouse, 1923, p. 9.

63 *Ibid.*, p. 28.
64 A. COWELL—A. MOSS SR.—W.J. C'HAIR, *Arapaho Stories, Songs, and Prayers: A Bilingual Anthology*, Norman, OK, University of Oklahoma, 2014, p. 267: story 'Open Brain'.
65 *Ibid.*, p. 212.
66 L.D. LINFORD, *Navajo Places: History, Legend, Landscape: A Narrative of Important Places on and Near the Navajo Reservation, with Notes on Their Significance to Navajo Culture and History*, Salt Lake City, UT, University of Utah Press, 2000, s.v. "Mitten Peak".
67 C.L. SMITHSON—R.C. EULER, *Havasupai Legends: Religion and Mythology of the Havasupai Indians of the Grand Canyon*, Salt Lake City, UT, University of Utah Press, 1994, p. 2.
68 J.K. MCNELEY, *Holy Wind in Navajo Philosophy*, Tucson, AZ, University of Arizona Press, 1981, p. 1, quoting Navajo texts in his primary collection: for life, Texts 8–9, and for thought, Texts 9–13, 30, and 37–41.
69 *Ibid.*, pp. 17–18.
70 MCNELEY, *Holy Wind in Navajo Philosophy*, pp. 18–21.
71 *Ibid.*, p. 21.
72 R.D. MILLER II, *Many Roads Lead Eastward : Overtures to Catholic Biblical Theology*, Eugene, OR, Cascade, 2016.
73 For this value of Reception History, see I. BOXALL, *Patmos in the Reception History of the Apocalypse* (Oxford Theology and Religion Monographs), Oxford, Oxford University Press, 2013, p. 9.
74 F. MITHRIDATES, *The Book of Bahir: Flavius Mithridates' Latin Translation, the Hebrew Text and an English Version* (The Kabbalistic Library of Giovanni Pico della Mirandola, 2), trans. S. Campanini, Turin, Aragno, 2005, pp. 12–13, 81, 338–339.
75 E. STAROBINSKI-SAFRAN, *L'Image du désert dans le Midrache*, in Y. CHRISTE (ed.), *Le Désert: image et réalité* (Les Cahiers du CEPOA, 3), Leuven, Peeters, 1989, 161–171, p. 161.

Notes to The Folkloric Desert

76 STAROBINSKI-SAFRAN, L'Image du désert dans le Midrache, p. 162.
77 MCGINN, Ocean and Desert as Symbols, p. 156.
78 J.-Y. LELOUP, Désert, déserts, Paris, Albin Michel, 2000, p. 45.
79 K. REDICK, Spiritual Rambling: Long Distance Wilderness Sojourning as Meaning-Making, in Journal of Ritual Studies 30 (2016) 41–52; D. JASPER, The Sacred Desert: Religion, Literature, Art, and Culture, Malden, MA, Blackwell, 2004; LELOUP, Désert, déserts, pp. 60–63.
80 LINDEMANN, Die Wüste, p. 69.
81 J. WERNER, Mit Sehnsucht und Seelengepack in die Unendlichkeit, in Publik-Forum Extra: Magazin für Spiritualität und Lebenskunst (October 2007) 12–14, p. 14; C. CORDONI, The Desert as Locus Dei in Barlaam and Josaphat?, in Cahiers de recherches médiévales et humanistes 18 (2009) 389–400, pp. 389–390.
82 LINDEMANN, Die Wüste, p. 70.
83 M. HOFER, Francis for Men: Otherwise We Need Weapons, Cincinnati, OH, St. Anthony Messenger, 2003, pp. 75–76; GRESHAKE, Die Wüste bestehen, p. 40.
84 T. ANDRÆ, In the Garden of Myrtles: Studies in Early Islamic Mysticism (SUNY Series in Muslim Spirituality in South Asia), Albany, NY, State University of New York Press, 1987, p. 12.
85 C.G. JUNG, The Red Book = Liber Novus, New York, NY, W.W. Norton, 2012, pp. 141–143, 145.
86 WALTERS, Soul Wilderness, pp. 3, 59.
87 MCGINN, Ocean and Desert as Symbols, p. 160; GRESHAKE, Spiritualität der Wüste, p. 112.
88 WILLIAMS, Wilderness and Paradise in Christian Thought, pp. 50–52; M. EGERDING, Die Metaphorik der spätmittelalterlichen Mystik, 2 vols., Paderborn, Ferdinand Schöningh, 1997, p. 2.722; also William of Saint-Thierry, David of Augsburg, Conrad of Eberbach, Gilbert of Hoyland, and Isaac of Stella; MCGINN, Ocean and Desert as Symbols, pp. 164–165.

Notes to *The Folkloric Desert*

89 J. HÄMEEN-ANTTILA, *Journey through the Desert, Journey towards God,* in *Journal of the Muhyiddin ibn Arabi Society* 37 (2005) 99–125.
90 Cited in COMINS, *A Wild Faith,* p. 172.
91 E.g., in his authentic works, Sermon *Of the Nobleman; Predigt* 10; *Predigt* 12; *Predigt* 48; *Predigt* 60; *Predigt* 81.
92 Perhaps pseudepigraphal, but from his circle.
93 W. BURKERT, *The Temple in Classical Greece,* in *Temple in Society,* ed. Michael V. Fox, Winona Lake: Eisenbrauns, 1988, p. 36.
94 B. D. SMITH, *The Indescribable God: Divine Otherness in Christian Theology,* Eugene: Pickwick Publications, 2012, p. 40.
95 Lindemann, *Die Wüste,* p. 88; J.-Y. Leloup, *Désert, déserts,* Paris: Albin Michel, 2000, pp. 68–69; McGinn, "Ocean and Desert," pp. 161–62, 166; Williams, *Wilderness and Paradise in Christian Thought,* p. 52; S. Coakley, *Re-Thinking Dionysius the Areopagite,* in *Modern Theology* 24 (2008) 531–32.
96 McGinn, *Ocean and Desert,* 162; Eriugena was the first to translate Pseudo-Dionysius into Latin, and Eckhart depended on him (and Dionysius) in many other areas, as well; M. Brennan, *Guide des Études érigéniennes: Bibliographie Commentée des Publications 1930–1987 = A Guide to Eriugenian Studies* (Vestigia Études et Documents de Philosophie Antique et Médiévale 5) Fribourg: Fribourg University Press, 1989, pp. 132, 294.
97 J. SCOT, *Commentaire Sur l'Evangile de Jean,* trans. E. JEAUNEAU (Sources Chretiennes 180) Paris: Cerf, 1972, pp. 140–42 n.18.
98 K. A. GORDON, *Traces in the Desert: The Poetics of Sand, Dust, and Ash in German Literature,* Diss., University of California, Berkeley, 2014, p. 9.
99 P. A. DIETRICK, *The Wilderness of God in Hadewijch II and Meister Eckhart and His Circle,* in *Meister Eckhart and the Beguine Mystics: Hadewijch of Brabant, Mechthild of*

Notes to *Caveats*

Magdeburg, and Marguerite Porete, ed. B. MCGINN, New York: Continuum, 1994, pp. 33, 35–36, 38–39; JOHN OF RUYSBROECK, *Les noces spirituelles*, trans. A. LOUF, Bégrolles-en-Mauges: Abbaye de Bellefontaine, 1993, p. 221; LANE, *The Solace of Fierce Landscapes*, p. 49.
100 BAHA'U'LLAH, *The Seven Valleys and the Four Valleys*, Wilmette, IL, Bahá'í Publishing Trust, 1968.

VIII
Caveats

1 Q. SKINNER, *Meaning and Understanding in the History of Ideas*, in *History and Ideas* 8 (1969) 3–53, pp. 24, 27–28.
2 E.g., G. GRAFF, JR.—E.R. BALL, *Till the Sands of the Desert Grow Cold* (Historic Sheet Music Collection), M. Witmark & Sons, 1911, Paper 1514; online: http://digitalcommons.conncoll.edu/sheetmusic/1514. Nevertheless, as ZIMMERMANN, *The Jungle and the Aroma of Meats*, p. ix, writes, 'Literature (Fennimore Cooper, Longfellow, Thoreau, and so on) should not obscure the historical truth which, as early as the late eighteenth century, the "philosophers" clearly perceived': a despising of the wilderness and glorification of man who tamed and replaced it.
3 L. HAZLETON, *Where Mountains Roar: A Personal Report from the Sinai and Negev Deserts*, 1st ed., New York, NY, Holt, Rinehart, Winston, 1980, p. 138.
4 *Ibid.*, p. 47.
5 LINDEMANN, *Die Wüste*, p. 13; HALEN—LECLERQ, *Désert et altérite*, p. 24.
6 J.B. CALLICOTT—M.P. NELSON, eds., *The Great New Wilderness Debate*, Athens, GA, University of Georgia, 1998, p. 5—the essay reprinted on pp. 201–206; also VUCETICH—NELSON, *Distinguishing Experiential and Physical Conceptions*, p. 616. HAZLETON, *Where Mountains Roar*, p. 47, uses the phrase 'unsullied by human activity' for a land Bedouin have inhabited for centuries.
7 CALLICOTT—NELSON, *The Great New Wilderness Debate*,

Notes to Conclusion

p. 6—the essay reprinted on pp. 231–245; also K. DeLuca— A. Demo, *Imagining Nature and Erasing Class and Race*, in M.P. Nelson—J.B. Callicott (eds.), *The Wilderness Debate Rages On*, Athens, GA, University of Georgia Press, 2008, 189–217, p. 208.

8 Callicott—Nelson, *The Great New Wilderness Debate*, pp. 7–9; G.W. Foreman, *The Real Wilderness Idea*, in M.P. Nelson—J.B. Callicott (eds.), *The Wilderness Debate Rages On*, Athens, GA, University of Georgia Press, 2008, pp. 378–397.

9 Johnson, *Ideas of landscape*, p. 27; Callicott—Nelson, *The Great New Wilderness Debate*, p. 19.

10 Abbey, *Desert solitaire*, p. 167; C. Quarch, *Goldene Wellen im Abendlicht*, in *Publik-Forum Extra: Magazin für Spiritualität und Lebenskunst* (October 2007) 3–5, p. 5.

11 Abbey, *Desert solitaire*, pp. 167–168.

12 McGinn, *Ocean and Desert as Symbols*, pp. 155–156, a view shared by Hazleton, *Where Mountains Roar*, p. 170 and, Lane, *The Solace of Fierce Landscapes*, pp. 14–15.

13 Andræ, *In the Garden of Myrtles*, pp. 14–15; C. Sahner, *Islamic Legends about the Birth of Monasticism*, in R. G. Hoyland (ed.), *The Late Antique World of Early Islam*, Princeton, NJ, Darwin, 2015, 393–435, p. 410.

14 Sahner, *Islamic Legends*, pp. 400–405, 410.

15 *Ibid.*, pp. 421–423.

16 X. Planhol, *Le désert, cadre géographique de l'expérience religieuse*, in *Les Mystiques du désert dans l'Islam, le judaïsme et le christianisme*, Gordes, France, Association des Amis de Sénanque, 1975, 5–16, p. 6.

17 Abbey, *Desert solitaire*, p. 184.

18 *Ibid.*, p. 213.

IX
Conclusion

1 Walters, *Soul Wilderness*, pp. 61–64.

2 Greshake, *Spiritualität der Wüste*, p. 34; Coetzee, *Wild God in the Wilderness*, pp. 88–89, 310.

Notes to *Conclusion*

3   COETZEE, *Wild God in the Wilderness*, p. 319.
4   COMINS, *Wilderness Spirituality*, p. 4; COMINS, *A Wild Faith*, p. 25.
5   M. ROBBINS, *The Desert-Mountain Experience*, in *Journal of Pastoral Care* 35 (1981) 18–35, p. 22; GRESHAKE, *Eine Landschaft*, p. 39; FLECKENSTEIN, *Botschaft der Wüste*, p. 116. One doesn't need to know the desert God; the desert simply 'is' and is not meant to be mapped or named. One merely sits within the fearsome awe; T.T. WILLIAMS, *Refuge: an unnatural history of family and place*, 2nd ed., New York, NY, Vintage Books, 2001, p. 148.
6   COETZEE, *Wild God in the Wilderness*, p. 312.
7   LINDEMANN, *Die Wüste*, p. 63.
8   GRESHAKE, *Eine Landschaft*, p. 21; GRESHAKE, *Spiritualität der Wüste*, pp. 31, 35; GRESHAKE, *Die Wüste bestehen*, p. 39; COMINS, *A Wild Faith*, p. 28.
9   HUXLEY, *The Desert*, p. 73.
10 LANE, *The Solace of Fierce Landscapes*, p. 99; cf. GRESHAKE, *Spiritualität der Wüste*, p. 35; GRESHAKE, *Eine Landschaft*, p. 21; COETZEE, *Wild God in the Wilderness*, pp. 89, 306.
11 HUXLEY, *The Desert*, p. 74; WALTERS, *Soul Wilderness*, p. 2.
12 ROBBINS, *Desert-Mountain Experience*, p. 23.
13 KRUTCH, *Voice of the Desert*, p. 222.
14 JUNG, *Approaching the Unconscious*, p. 21.
15 GUÉNON, *Fundamental Symbols*, p. 14.
16 STEIN, *Jung's Map of the Soul*, p. 100.
17 BORELLA, *The Crisis of Religious Symbolism*, p. 3.
18 BORELLA, *The Crisis of Religious Symbolism*, p. 3.
19 *Ibid.*, p. 4.
20 CASSIRER, *Language and Myth*, p. 87.
21 SZLAMOWICZ, *Food, memory and the blues*, p. 33.
22 J.L. HENDERSON, *Ancient myths and modern man*, in C.G. JUNG—M.-L. FRANZ (eds.), *Man and his Symbols*, Garden City, NY, Doubleday, 1964, 104–157, p. 106. The only other traditional hymnic setting of the Yahweh-from-the-South biblical poetic fragments is #21 in R. BELL—J.C. HOATSON, *The Halifax Selection of Hymns*, Halifax, Whilley

Notes to *Conclusion*

& Booth, 1824, by "L.M.", "From Teman came the Mighty God, The Holy One from Paran Hill; The nations trembled at his nod, Checked in its course the sun stood still"; but this hymn is more narrative than mythic, describing biblical events and God's triumph over pestilence and sinners.

BIBLIOGRAPHY

Abbey, E. *Desert solitaire: A season in the wilderness*. London: Clark, 1992.

Ahmed, M. T., ed. *Ecosystems and Human Well-Being: El Maghara, Northern Sinai, Egypt*. Nairobi: UNEP, 2010.

Aldenderfer, M. 'Envisioning a pragmatic approach to the archaeology of religion'. Pages 23–36 in *Beyond Belief: The Archaeology of Religion and Ritual*. Edited by Y. M. Rowan. Archaeological Papers of the American Anthropological Association 21. Hoboken: American Anthropological Association, 2012.

Andræ, T. *In the Garden of Myrtles: Studies in Early Islamic Mysticism*. SUNY Series in Muslim Spirituality in South Asia. Albany: State University of New York Press, 1987.

Anttonen, V. 'Landscapes as Sacroscapes'. Pages 13–32 in *Sacred Sites and Holy Places: Exploring the Sacralization of Landscape through Space and Time*. Edited by S. W. Nordeide. Studies in the Early Middle Ages 11. Turnhout: Brepols, 2013.

Ármann Jakobsson. 'The Trollish Acts of Thorgrimr the Witch'. *Saga-Book* 32 (2008): 39–66.

Avni, Y., N. Porat, and G. Avni. 'Pre-farming environment and OSL Chronology in the Negev Highlands, Israel'. *Journal of Arid Environments* 86 (2012): 12–27.

Bahá'u'lláh. *The Seven Valleys and the Four Valleys*. Wilmette: Baha'i Publishing Trust, 1968.

Barr, J. 'Migraš in the Old Testament'. *Journal of Semitic Studies* 29 (1984): 15–31.

Basso, K. H. *Wisdom Sits in Places: Landscape and language among the Western Apache*. Albuquerque: University of New Mexico Press, 1996.

Bibliography

Baudrillard, J. *America*. London: Verso, 2010.

Benveniste, E. 'L'appareil formel de l'énonciation'. *Langages* 5, no. 17 (1970): 12–18.

Berezkin, Y. 'Folklore and Mythology Catalogue'. *Retrospective Methods Network Newsletter* 10 (2015): 58–70.

Birrell, A., ed. *The Classic of Mountains and Seas*. Penguin Classics. London: Penguin Putnam, 1999.

Borella, J. *The Crisis of Religious Symbolism & Symbolism and Reality*. Translated by G. J. Champoux. Kettering, Ohio: Angelico, 2016.

Borrie, W. T., and J. W. Roggenbuck. 'The Dynamic, Emergent, and Multi-Phasic Nature of On-Site Wilderness Experiences'. *Journal of Leisure Research* 33 (2001): 202–28.

Bourdieu, P. *Outline of a theory of practice* (1972). 25th ed. Cambridge Studies in Social and Cultural Anthropology 16. Cambridge, UK: Cambridge University Press, 2010.

Boxall, I. *Patmos in the Reception History of the Apocalypse*. Oxford Theology and Religion Monographs. Oxford: Oxford University Press, 2013.

Brawley, C. *Nature and the Numinous in Mythopoeic Fantasy Literature*. Critical Explorations in Science Fiction and Fantasy 46. Jefferson, N.C.: McFarland, 2014.

Bremmer, J. N. 'Greek Demons of the Wilderness'. Pages 25–54 in *Wilderness in Mythology and Religion: Approaching Religious Spatialities, Cosmologies, and Ideas of Wild Nature*. Edited by L. Feldt. Religion and Society 55. Boston: De Gruyter, 2012.

Brodkey, L. 'Writing Ethnographic Narratives'. *Written Communication* 4 (1987): 25–50.

Brook, I. 'Goethean Science as a Way to Read Landscape'. *Landscape Research* 23 (1998): 51–69.

Brough, J. 'Audumbarāyaṇa's Theory of Language'. *Bulletin of the School of Oriental and African Studies, University of London* 14 (1952): 73–77.

Brydone, P., W. Beckford, and J. F. Junius. *P. Brydone's Reise durch Sicilien und Malta, in Briefen an William Beckford. Esq.*

Bibliography

zu Somerly in Suffolk: nebst einer Charte von Sicilien und Malta. Leipzig: Bey Johann Friedrich Junius, 1777.

Bryson, B. *A walk in the woods*. London: Corgi, 1998.

Burckhardt, T. *Mirror of the intellect: Essays on traditional science & sacred art*. SUNY Series in Islam. Albany: State University of New York Press, 1987.

Burden, T. L. *The Kerygma of the Wilderness Traditions in the Hebrew Bible*. American University Studies Theology and Religion Series 7.163. New York: Peter Lang, 1994.

Burnett, G. W., R. Joulie-Kuttner, and K. Kang'ethe. 'A Willing Benefactor: An Essay on Wilderness in Nilotic and Bantu Culture'. Pages 282–99 in *The Wilderness Debate Rages on: Continuing the Great New Wilderness Debate*. Edited by M. P. Nelson and J. B. Callicott. Athens, Ga.: University of Georgia Press, 2008.

Burnett, G. W., and K. W. Kang'ethe. 'Wilderness and the Bantu Mind'. *Environmental Ethics* 16 (1994): 145–60.

Callicott, J. B., and M. P. Nelson, eds. *The Great New Wilderness Debate*. Athens, Ga.: University of Georgia, 1998.

Carroll, A. N. 'Religious Symbolism, Jungian Archetypal Theory, and an Encounter with Evil'. PhD diss., The Catholic University of America, Washington, DC, 2012.

Cassirer, E. *Language and Myth* (1925). New York: Dover, 1953.

Chalevelaki, M. 'Présence de l'objet et identité des marques de luxe : approche socio-sémiotique'. PhD diss., Université Lumière Lyon 2, 2007.

Coetzee, N. J. 'Wild God in the Wilderness: Why does Yahweh choose to appear in the Wilderness in the Book of Exodus?' PhD Diss., University of Birmingham, Birmingham, 2016.

Comins, M. *A Wild Faith: Jewish Ways into Wilderness, Wilderness Ways into Judaism*. Woodstock, Vt.: Jewish Lights Publishing, 2007.

———. 'Wilderness Spirituality'. *CCAR Journal: A Reform Jewish Quarterly* 53 (2006): 3–9.

Cordoni, C. 'The Desert as locus Dei in Barlaam and Josaphat?' *Cahiers de recherches médiévales et humanistes* 18 (2009): 389–400.

Bibliography

Cowell, A., A. Moss Sr., and W. J. C'Hair. *Arapaho Stories, Songs, and Prayers: A Bilingual Anthology*. Norman, Ok.: University of Oklahoma, 2014.

Crane, K. 'Wilderness Effects and Wild Affects in UK Nature/Travel Writing'. Pages 41–57 in *English Topographies in Literature and Culture*. Edited by I. Habermann and D. Keller. Vol. 23. Spatial Practices 23. Leiden: Brill, 2016.

Crist, E. 'Against the Social Construction of Nature and Wilderness'. Pages 500–525 in *The Wilderness Debate Rages on: Continuing the Great New Wilderness Debate*. Edited by M. P. Nelson and J. B. Callicott. Athens, Ga: University of Georgia Press, 2008.

Crumley, C. L. 'Exploring the Venues of Social Memory'. Pages 39–52 in *Social Memory and History: Anthropological Perspectives*. Edited by J. Climo and M. G. Cattell. Walnut Creek, Calif.: Altamira, 2002.

Cunningham, P. L., and T. Wronski. 'Arabian Wolf Distribution Update from Saudi Arabia'. *Canid News* 13 (2010). No pages. Online: https://www.canids.org/canidnews/13/Arabian_wolf_in_Saudi_Arabia.pdf.

Danin, A. *Plants of Desert dunes*. Adaptations of Desert Organisms. New York: Springer, 1996.

Davenport, G. *The Geography of the Imagination Forty Essays*. Boston: David R. Godine, 2005.

De Pury, A. 'L'image du désert dans l'Ancien Testament'. Pages 115–26 in *Le Désert: image et réalité*. Edited by Y. Christe. Les Cahiers du CEPOA 3. Leuven: Peeters, 1989.

Debord, G. 'Introduction to a Critique of Urban Geography'. *Les Lèvres Nues*, 1955. No pages. Online: http://library.nothingness.org/articles/SI/en/display/2.

———. 'Theory of the Dérive'. *Les Lèvres Nues*, November 1959. No pages. Online: www.cddc.vt.edu/sionline/si/theory.html.

DeLuca, K., and A. Demo. 'Imagining Nature and Erasing Class and Race'. Pages 189–217 in *The Wilderness Debate Rages on: Continuing the Great New Wilderness Debate*. Edited by

Bibliography

M. P. Nelson and J. B. Callicott. Athens, Ga: University of Georgia Press, 2008.

Duncan, N., and J. Duncan. 'Doing Landscape Interpretation'. Pages 225–47 in *The Sage Handbook of Qualitative Geography*. Edited by D. DeLyser, S. Herbert, S. Aitken, M. Crang, and L. McDowell. Los Angeles: Sage, 2010.

Egeler, M. 'A Retrospective Methodology for Using Landnamabok as a Source for the Religious History of Iceland?' *Retrospective Methods Network Newsletter* 10 (2015): 78–92.

Egerding, M. *Die Metaphorik der spätmittelalterlichen Mystik.* Vol. 2. Paderborn, Germany: Ferdinand Schöningh, 1997.

Eisenberg, J. F. 'The Behavior Patterns of Desert Rodents'. Pages 189–224 in *Rodents in Desert Environments*. Edited by I. Prakash and P. K. Ghosh. Monographiae biologicae 28. The Hague: Junk, 1975.

Evans-Pritchard, E. E. 'Fieldwork and the Empirical Tradition' (1951). Vol. 1, pages 103–15 in *Fieldwork*. Sage Benchmarks in Social Research Methods. Thousand Oaks: Sage, 2005.

———. 'Some reminiscences and reflections on fieldwork (Appendix IV)'. Pages 240–54 in *Witchcraft, Oracles, and Magic among the Azande*. Edited by E. E. Evans-Pritchard and E. Gillies. Oxford: Clarendon, 1976.

Fagg, C. W., A. Greaves, and K. Langdon. *Acacia Tortilis: 1925–1988. Annotated Bibliography / CAB F41*. Oxford: CAB International, 1990.

Feldt, L. 'Religion, Nature, and Ambiguous Space in Ancient Mesopotamia: The Mountain Wilderness in Old Babylonian Religious Narratives'. *Numen* 63 (2016): 347–82.

———. 'Wilderness and Hebrew Bible Religion'. Pages 55–94 in *Wilderness in Mythology and Religion: Approaching Religious Spatialities, Cosmologies, and Ideas of Wild Nature*. Edited by L. Feldt. Religion and Society 55. Boston: De Gruyter, 2012.

Fibiger, M. C. Q. 'Wilderness as Necessary Feature in Hindu Religion'. Pages 131–56 in *Wilderness in Mythology and Religion: Approaching Religious Spatialities, Cosmologies,*

Bibliography

and Ideas of Wild Nature. Edited by L. Feldt. Religion and Society 55. Boston: De Gruyter, 2012.

Filser, J., and R. Prasse. 'A Glance on the Fauna of Nizzana'. Pages 125–48 in *Arid Dune Ecosystems: The Nizzana Sands in the Negev Desert*. Edited by S. W. Breckle, A. Yāʿîr, and M. Veste. Ecological Studies 200. Berlin: Springer, 2008.

Firmage, E. 'Zoology'. *Anchor Bible Dictionary*. Garden City: Doubleday & Co., 1992.

Flavius Mithridates. *The Book of Bahir: Flavius Mithridates' Latin Translation, the Hebrew Text and an English Version*. Translated by S. Campanini. The Kabbalistic Library of Giovanni Pico della Mirandola 2. Turin: Aragno, 2005.

Fleckenstein, K.-H. *Botschaft der Wüste*. Innsbruck: Tyrolia-Verlag, 2016.

Foreman, G. W. 'The Real Wilderness Idea'. Pages 378–97 in *The Wilderness Debate Rages on: Continuing the Great New Wilderness Debate*. Edited by M. P. Nelson and J. B. Callicott. Athens, Ga: University of Georgia Press, 2008.

Franz, M.-L. von. *Archetypal Dimensions of the Psyche*. Boston: Shambhala, 1997.

Friedenberg, J., and G. Silverman. *Cognitive Science: An Introduction to the Study of Mind*. 2nd ed. Los Angeles: Sage, 2012.

Frog. 'Mythology in Cultural Practice: A Methodological Framework for Historical Analysis'. *Retrospective Methods Network Newsletter* 10 (2015): 33–57.

Geertz, C. 'Being There (1988)'. Vol. 4, pages 127–40 in *Fieldwork*. Edited by C. Pole. Sage Benchmarks in Social Research Methods. Thousand Oaks: Sage, 2005.

———. '"From the Native's Point of View": On the Art of Anthropological Understanding'. *Bulletin of the American Academy of Arts and Sciences* 28 (1974): 26–45.

———. 'Thick description: Toward an interpretive theory of culture'. Pages 3–30 in *The Interpretation of Cultures*. New York: Basic Books, 1973.

Gemeinboeck, P. 'Impossible Geographies'. in *Intensive Science*. Exhibition catalogue. Paris: Sony CSL, 2006.

Bibliography

George Graff, Jr., and E. R. Ball. 'Till the Sands of the Desert Grow Cold'. M. Witmark & Sons, 1911. Paper 1514. Historic Sheet Music Collection. No pages. Online: http://digitalcommons.conncoll.edu/sheetmusic/1514.

Goodwyn, E. 'Recurrent Motifs as Resonant Attractor States in the Narrative Field'. *Journal of Analytic Psychology* 58 (2013): 387–408.

Gray, A. R. *Psalm 18 in Words and Pictures: A Reading Through Metaphor*. Biblical Interpretation Series 127. Leiden: Brill, 2014.

Gregoire, J. 'Du Khamsin et des ses effets'. *Mémoires ou travaux originaux présentés et lus à l'Institut égyptien* 1 (1862): 369–82.

Greshake, G. *Die Wüste bestehen: Erlebnis und geistliche Erfahrung*. Kevelaer, Germany: Verlagsgemeinschaft Topos plus, 2004.

———. 'Eine Landschaft wie das Leben'. *Publik-Forum Extra: Magazin für Spiritualität und Lebenskunst*, October 2007.

———. *Spiritualität der Wüste*. Innsbruck: Tyrolia-Verl, 2002.

Guénon, R. *Fundamental Symbols*. Oxford: Alden, 1962.

Gunnell, T. 'How Elvish were the Alfar?' Pages 111–30 in *Constructing Nations, Reconstructing Myth*. Edited by A. Wawn. Making the Middle Ages 9. Turnhout: Brepols, 2007.

———. 'Nordic Folk Legends, Folk Traditions and Grave Mounds'. Pages 17–41 in *New Focus on Retrospective Methods: Resuming Methodological Discussions: Case Studies from Northern Europe*. Edited by E. Heide and K. Bek-Pedersen. Folklore Fellows' Communications 307. Helsinki: Suomalainen Tiedeakatemia, Academia Scientiarum Fennica, 2014.

Haaland, R., and G. Haaland. 'Landscape'. Pages 24–37 in *The Oxford Handbook of the Archaeology of Ritual and Religion*. Edited by T. Insoll. Oxford Handbooks. Oxford: Oxford University Press, 2011.

Habermann, I. 'Running Rings Round London: Psychogeography in Iain Sinclair's London Orbital'. Pages 61–73 in *English*

Bibliography

Topographies in Literature and Culture. Edited by I. Habermann and D. Keller. Spatial Practices 23. Leiden: Brill, 2016.

Haldar, A. 'The Notion of the Desert in Sumero-Accadian and West-Semitic Religions'. *Uppsala Universitets Årsskrif* 3 (1950): 11–70.

Halen, P., and E. Leclerq. 'Désert et altérite'. Pages 11–30 in *Le désert, un espace paradoxal*. Edited by G. Nauroy, P. Halen, and A.-E. Spica. Recherches en littérature et spiritualité vol. 2. Bern: Lang, 2003.

Hall, T. E., and D. N. Cole. 'Immediate Conscious Experience in Wilderness'. Pages 37–49 in *Wilderness Visitor Experiences*. Edited by D. N. Cole. USDA Forest Service Proceedings RMRS-P-66. Missoula, Mont.: US Department of Agriculture, 2012.

Hämeen-Anttila, J. 'Journey through the Desert, Journey towards God'. *Journal of the Muhyiddin Ibn Arabi Society* 37 (2005): 99–125.

Harir, S. 'Adaptive Forms and Process Among the Hadendowa'. Pages 81–102 in *Survival on Meagre Resources: Hadendowa Pastoralism in the Red Sea Hills*. Edited by L. O. Manger. Uppsala: Nordiska Afrikainstitutet, 1996.

Harrison, D. L. *The Mammals of Arabia*. Vol. 2. London: Ernest Benn, 1968.

Hazleton, L. *Where Mountains Roar: A Personal Report from the Sinai and Negev Deserts*. New York: Holt, Rinehart, Winston, 1980.

Held, C. C. *Middle East Patterns: Places, Peoples, and Politics*. 3rd ed. Boulder: Westview, 2000.

Henderson, J. L. 'Ancient myths and modern man'. Pages 104–57 in *Man and His Symbols*. Edited by C. G. Jung and M.-L. Franz. Garden City, N.Y.: Doubleday, 1964.

Hofer, M. *Francis for Men: Otherwise We Need Weapons*. Cincinnati: St. Anthony Messenger, 2003.

Hoffmann, T. 'Notes on Qur'anic Wisdom'. Pages 157–82 in *Wilderness in Mythology and Religion: Approaching Religious*

Bibliography

Spatialities, Cosmologies, and Ideas of Wild Nature. Edited by L. Feldt. Religion and Society 55. Boston: De Gruyter, 2012.

Holdrege, C. 'Doing Goethean Science'. *Janus Head* 8 (2005): 27–52.

Holm, I. 'A Cultural Landscape beyond the Infield/Outfield Categories'. *Norwegian Archaeological Review* 35 (2002): 67–80.

Honko, L. 'Memorates and the Study of Folk Beliefs'. *Journal of the Folklore Institute* 1 (1964): 5–19.

Hopkins, W. D. 'Laterality in Maternal Cradling and Infant Positional Biases: Implications for the Development and Evolution of Hand Preferences in Nonhuman Primates'. *International Journal of Primatology* 25 (2004): 1243–65.

Hoppal, M. 'Linguistic and Mental Models for Hungarian Folk Beliefs'. Pages 50–66 in *Myth and Mentality: Studies in Folklore and Popular Thought*. Edited by A.-L. Siikala. Studia Fennica folkloristica / Suomalaisen Kirjallisuuden Seura 8. Helsinki: Finnish Literature Society, 2002.

Huxley, A. 'The Desert'. *Adonis and the Alphabet*. London: Chatto & Windus, 1956.

Hymes, D. *Foundations in Sociolinguistics*. Philadelphia: University of Pennsylvania Press, 1974.

Insoll, T. *Archaeology, Ritual, Religion*. New York: Routledge, 2004.

Jabbūr, J. S. *The Bedouins and the Desert: Aspects of Nomadic Life in the Arab East*. SUNY Series in Near Eastern Studies. Albany: State University of New York Press, 1995.

Jasper, D. *The Sacred Desert: Religion, Literature, Art, and Culture*. Malden, Mass.: Blackwell, 2004.

Johnson, M. *Ideas of landscape*. Oxford: Blackwell, 2007.

Jung, C. G. 'Approaching the unconscious'. Pages 18–103 in *Man and His Symbols*. Edited by C. G. Jung and M.-L. von Franz. Garden City, N.Y.: Doubleday, 1964.

———. *The Red Book = Liber Novus*. New York: Norton, 2012.

Kari, J. M., J. A. Fall, S. Pete, and M. Alex, eds. *Shem Pete's Alaska: The Territory of the Upper Cook Inlet Dena'ina*. 2nd ed. Fairbanks, Alaska: University of Alaska Press, 2003.

Bibliography

Kelly, M. H., and F. C. Keil. 'Metaphor Comprehension and Knowledge of Semantic Domains'. Pages 511–28 in *Metaphor and Figurative Language*. Edited by P. Hanks and R. Giora. Critical concepts in linguistics 3. Abingdon, United Kingdom: Routledge, 2012.

Koppen, W. P., and R. Geiger. *Klima der Erde = Climate of the Earth*. Darmstadt: Justus Perthes, 1985.

Kouri, J. 'Co-Composing a Village History in the Archipelago of South-western Finland'. Pages 231–50 in *The Relational Dynamics of Disenchantment and Sacralization: Changing the Terms of the Religion versus Secularity Debate*. Edited by P. Ingman. The Study of Religion in a Global Context. Bristol, Conn.: Equinox Publishing, 2016.

Krutch, J. W. *The Voice of the Desert: A Naturalist's Interpretation*. New York: William Sloane, 1966.

Lackenbacher, S. 'L'image du désert d'apreès les textes littéraires assyro-babyloniens'. Pages 57–65 in *Le Désert: Image et réalité*. Edited by Y. Christe. Les cahiers du CEPOA 3. Leuven: Peeters, 1989.

Lane, B. C. *The Solace of Fierce Landscapes: Exploring Desert and Mountain Spirituality*. New York: Oxford University Press, 1998.

Larrington, C., trans. *The Poetic Edda*. Oxford World's Classics. Oxford: Oxford University Press, 2008.

Lawlor, D. 'Returning to Wirikuta'. *European Journal of Ecopsychology* 4 (2013): 19–31.

Lawrence, T. E. *Seven Pillars of Wisdom*. London: Jonathan Cape, 1935.

Leal, R. B. 'Negativity toward Wilderness in the Biblical Record'. *Ecotheology* 10 (2005): 364–81.

———. *Wilderness in the Bible: Toward a theology of wilderness*. Studies in Biblical Literature 72. New York: P. Lang, 2004.

Lebrun, R. 'Les Hittites et le désert'. Pages 81–88 in *Le Désert: image et réalité*. Edited by Y. Christe. Les cahiers du CEPOA 3. Leuven: Peeters, 1989.

Lee, W. W. 'The Concept of the Wilderness in the Pentateuch'. Pages 1–16 in *Israel in the Wilderness: Interpretations of the*

Bibliography

Biblical Naratives in Jewish and Christian Traditions. Edited by K. E. Pomykala. Themes in Biblical Narrative 10. Leiden: Brill, 2008.

Leloup, J.-Y. *Désert, déserts.* Paris: Albin Michel, 2000.

Lewis, C. S. 'Bluspels and Flalansferes: A Semantic Nightmare'. In *Rehabilitations and Other Essays.* London: Oxford University Press, 1939.

Lindemann, U. *Die Wüste: Terra incognita, Erlebnis, Symbol: eine Genealogie der abendländischen Wüstenvorstellungen in der Literatur von der Antike bis zur Gegenwart.* Beiträge zur neueren Literaturgeschichte 3.175. Heidelberg: Winter, 2000.

Linford, L. D. *Navajo Places: History, Legend, Landscape: A Narrative of Important Places on and Near the Navajo Reservation, with Notes on Their Significance to Navajo Culture and History.* Salt Lake City: University of Utah Press, 2000.

Lings, M. *Symbol & Archetype: A Study of the Meaning of Existence.* Louisville: Fons Vitae, 2006.

Littmann, T., and S. M. Berkowicz. 'The Regional Climatic Setting'. Pages 49–64 in *Arid Dune Ecosystems: The Nizzana Sands in the Negev Desert.* Edited by S. W. Breckle, A. Yā'îr, and M. Veste. Ecological Studies 200. Berlin: Springer, 2008.

Maingueneau, D. 'La situation d'enonciation entre langue et discours'. Pages 197–210 in *Dix ans de S.D.U.* Craiova, Romania: Editura Universitaria Craiova, 2004.

———. *L'Énonciation en linguistique française.* Les fondamentaux cycle 1.29. Paris: Hachette, 1996.

Malamoud, C. 'Village et foret dans l'ideologie de l'Inde brahmanique'. *European Journal of Sociology* 17 (1976): 3–20.

Malinowski, B. *Argonauts of the Western Pacific.* London: Routledge & Kegan Paul, 1922.

———. 'Method and Scope of Anthropological Fieldwork (1922)'. Pages 69–81 in *Ethnographic Fieldwork: An Anthropological Reader.* Edited by A. C. G. M. Robben and J. A. Sluka. 2nd ed. Blackwell Anthologies in Social and Cultural Anthropology. Malden, Mass.: Wiley-Blackwell, 2012.

Bibliography

Marks, J. S., D. L. Evans, and D. W. Holt. *Long-eared Owl*. The Birds of North America 33. Philadelphia: The Academy of Natural Sciences, 1994.

Mattoon, M. A. *Jung and the Human Psyche: An Understandable Introduction*. London: Routledge, 2005.

McGinn, B. 'Ocean and Desert as Symbols of Mystical Absorption in the Christian Tradition'. *The Journal of Religion* 74 (1994): 155–81.

McNeley, J. K. *Holy Wind in Navajo Philosophy*. Tuscon: University of Arizona Press, 1981.

Michaelis, C. B. *Hagiographos*. 3 vols. Halle, Germany: Orphanotrophei, 1720.

Miller, R. D., II. *Covenant and grace in the Old Testament: Assyrian propaganda and Israelite faith*. Perspectives on Hebrew Scriptures and its Contexts 16. Piscataway, NJ: Gorgias, 2012.

———. *Many roads lead eastward: Overtures to Catholic biblical theology*. Eugene, OR: Cascade, 2016.

Miquel, A. 'Le désert dans la poésie arabe préislamique'. Pages 73–88 in *Les Mystiques du désert dans l'Islam, le judaïsme et le christianisme*. Gordes, France: Association des Amis de Sénanque, 1975.

Montgomery, J. *Arabia and the Bible* (1934). New York: Ktav, 1969.

Moslund, S. P. 'The Presence of Place in Literature'. Pages 29–43 in *Geocritical Explorations: Space, Place, and Mapping in Literary and Cultural Studies*. Edited by R. T. Tally. New York: Palgrave Macmillan, 2011.

Nieuwenhuyse, D., J.-C. Génot, and D. H. Johnson. *The Little Owl: Conservation, Ecology and Behavior of Athene Noctua*. Cambridge, UK: Cambridge University Press, 2008.

Nyström, S. *Beduinentum und Jahwismus*. Lund: C. W. K. Gleerup, 1946.

O'Connor, M. P. 'Cardinal-Direction Terms in Biblical Hebrew'. Vol. 2, pages 1140–57 in *Semitic Studies*. Edited by A. S. Kaye. Wiesbaden, Germany: Harrassowitz, 1991.

Bibliography

Olden, S. *Shoshone Folk Lore*. Milwaukee: Morehouse, 1923.

Overall, S. 'The Walking Dead: or Why Psychogeography Matters'. Paper presented at the conference 'Re-Enchanting the Academy.' Canterbury, Christ Church University, 2015. No pages. Cited 4 January 2017. Online: https://www.canterbury.ac.uk/education/conferences-events/re-enchanting-the-academy/assets/sonia-overall.pdf.

Patterson, M. E., A. E. Watson, D. R. Williams, and J. W. Roggenbuck. 'An Hermeneutic Approach to Studying the Nature of Wilderness Experience'. *Journal of Leisure Research* 30 (1998): 423–52.

Pedersen, J. *Israel, Its Life and Culture*. London: Oxford University Press, 1926.

Planhol, X. 'Le désert, cadre géographique de l'expérience religieuse'. Pages 5–16 in *Les Mystiques du désert dans l'Islam, le judaïsme et le christianisme*. Gordes, France: Association des Amis de Sénanque, 1975.

Quarch, C. 'Goldene Wellen im Abendlicht'. *Publik-Forum Extra: Magazin für Spiritualität und Lebenskunst*, October 2007.

Quinn, N. 'The Cultural Basis of Metaphor (1991)'. Pages 133–63 in *Metaphor and Figurative Language*. Edited by P. Hanks and R. Giora. Critical concepts in Linguistics 3. Abingdon, United Kingdom: Routledge, 2012.

Qumsiyeh, M. B. *Mammals of the Holy Land*. Lubbock: Texas Tech University Press, 1996.

Redick, K. 'Spiritual Rambling: Long Distance Wilderness Sojourning as Meaning-Making'. *Journal of Ritual Studies* 30 (2016): 41–52.

Reid, T. *Essays on the Intellectual Powers of Man*. Cambridge, Mass.: MIT Press, 1813.

Robbins, M. 'The Desert-Mountain Experience'. *Journal of Pastoral Care* 35 (1981): 18–35.

Roccati, A. 'La conception rituelle du désert chez les ancien Egyptiens'. Pages 127–30 in *Le Désert: image et réalité*. Edited by Y. Christe. Les cahiers du CEPOA 3. Leuven: Peeters, 1989.

Rossetti, J. J. H. 'Darkness in the Desert: Tradition and

Bibliography

Transgression in Ibrāhīm al-Kūnī's Ushb al-Layl'. *Journal of Arabic Literature* 42 (2011): 49–66.

Sahner, C. 'Islamic Legends about the Birth of Monasticism'. Pages 393–435 in *The Late Antique World of Early Islam*. Edited by R. G. Hoyland. Princeton: Darwin, 2015.

Sangha, H., and D. Malik. 'Observations on wintering Pallid Scops Owl Otus brucei at Zainabad, Little Rann of Kachchh, Surendranagar district, Gujarat'. *Indian Birds* 5 (2010): 176–77.

Sapir, E. 'Language and Environment'. *American Anthropologist* n.s. 14 (1912): 226–42.

Sävborg, D. 'Scandinavian Folk Legends and Icelandic Sagas'. Pages 76–88 in *New Focus on Retrospective Methods: Resuming Methodological Discussions: Case Studies from Northern Europe*. Edited by E. Heide and K. Bek-Pedersen. Folklore Fellows' Communications 307. Helsinki: Suomalainen Tiedeakatemia, Academia Scientiarum Fennica, 2014.

Schmeichel, W. 'The Wilderness in Old Testament Thought'. Pages 43–59 in *The Wilderness*. Edited by J. Spencer. Kalamazoo: Kalamazoo College Press, 1980.

Schwartz, M. S., and C. G. Schwartz. 'Problems in Participant Observation'. *American Journal of Sociology* 60 (1955): 343–53.

Scott, D. *The Long-Eared Owl*. London: Hawk and Owl Trust, 1997.

Self, W. *Psychogeography: Disentangling the Modern Conundrum of Psyche and Place*. New York: Bloomsbury, 2007.

Siikala, A.-L. 'Variation in the Incantation and Mythical Thinking'. *Journal of Folklore Research* 23 (1986): 187–200.

———. 'What Myths Tell about Past Finno-Ugric Modes of Thinking'. Pages 15–32 in *Myth and Mentality: Studies in Folklore and Popular Thought*. Edited by A.-L. Siikala. Studia Fennica Folkloristica / Suomalaisen Kirjallisuuden Seura 8. Helsinki: Finnish Literature Society, 2002.

Sivall, T. 'Sirocco in the Levant'. *Geografiska Annaler* 39 (1957): 114–42.

Bibliography

Skinner, Q. 'Meaning and Understanding in the History of Ideas'. *History and Ideas* 8 (1969): 3–53.

Smithson, C. L., and R. C. Euler. *Havasupai Legends: Religion and Mythology of the Havasupai Indians of the Grand Canyon*. Salt Lake City: University of Utah Press, 1994.

Snorri Sturluson. *Edda*. Translated by A. Faulkes. Everyman Classics 499. London: Dent, 1987.

Som, B. 'Toward a Cognitive Linguistics Understanding of Folk Narratives.' *Lokaratna* 4 (2011): n.p.

Starobinski-Safran, E. 'L'Image du désert dans le Midrache'. Pages 161–71 in *Le Désert: image et réalité*. Edited by Y. Christe. Les Cahiers du CEPOA 3. Leuven: Peeters, 1989.

Staubli, T. *Das Image der Nomaden im alten Israel und in der Ikonographie seiner sesshaften Nachbarn*. Orbis Biblicus et Orientalis 107. Freiburg, Switzerland: Universitätsverlag, 1991.

Stein, M. *Jung's Map of the Soul: An Introduction*. Chicago: Open Court, 1998.

Stocking George W., Jr. 'The Ethnographer's Magic—Fieldwork in British Anthropology from Tylor to Malinkowki'. Vol. 1, pages 218–63 in *Fieldwork*. Sage Benchmarks in Social Research Methods. Thousand Oaks: Sage, 2005.

Szlamowicz, J. 'Food, memory and the blues'. *Les Mots du Jazz*. Toulouse: Presses Universitaires du Midi, 2018.

Talmon, S. 'The "Desert Motif" in the Bible and in Qumran Literature'. Pages 31–64 in *Biblical Motifs*. Edited by A. Altmann. Studies and Texts 3. Cambridge, Mass.: Harvard University Press, 1966.

Tarazi, P. N. *The rise of scripture*. St. Paul: Orthodox Center for the Advancement of Biblical Studies, 2017.

Taylor, M. 'Swimming in the flax field, verða at gjalti, and related matters'. Pages 91–134 in *Frederic Amory in Memoriam: Old Norse-Icelandic Studies*. Edited by J. Lindow and G. Clark. North Pinehurst Press, 2015.

Thiselton, A. C. 'The Supposed Power of Words in the Biblical Writings'. *Journal of Theological Studies* n.s. 25 (1974): 283–99.

Bibliography

Tielborger, K., R. Prasse, and H. Leschner. 'The Flora of the Nizzana Research Site'. Pages 93–104 in *Arid Dune Ecosystems: The Nizzana Sands in the Negev Desert*. Edited by S. W. Breckle, A. Yā'îr, and M. Veste. Ecological Studies 200. Berlin: Springer, 2008.

Tilley, C. Y. *A Phenomenology of Landscape: Places, Paths, and Monuments*. Explorations in Anthropology. Oxford: Berg, 1994.

Toelken, B. *The Dynamics of Folklore*. Rev. ed. Logan, Utah: Utah State University Press, 1996.

Tristram, H. B. *The Natural History of the Bible*. 10th ed. London: SPCK, 1911.

Tuan, Y. *Space and Place: The Perspective of Experience*. Minneapolis: University of Minnesota Press, 1977.

Vauclair, J., and C. Scola. 'Infant-holding biases in mothers and affective symptoms during pregnancy and after delivery'. *Infant and Child Development* 18 (2009): 106–21.

Viṣṇuśarman. *The Five Discourses on Worldly Wisdom*. Translated by P. Olivelle. The Clay Sanskrit Library. New York: New York University Press, 2006.

Vucetich, J. A., and M. P. Nelson. 'Distinguishing Experiential and Physical Conceptions of Wilderness'. Pages 611–31 in *The Wilderness Debate Rages On: Continuing the Great New Wilderness Debate*. Edited by M. P. Nelson and J. B. Callicott. Athens, Ga.: University of Georgia Press, 2008.

Wall, L. 'Finding Identity in the Wilderness'. Pages 66–77 in *Meister Eckhart and the Beguine Mystics: Hadewijch of Brabant, Mechthild of Magdeburg, and Marguerite Porete*. Edited by B. McGinn. New York: Continuum, 1994.

Walters, K. S. *Soul Wilderness: A Desert Spirituality*. New York: Paulist Press, 2001.

Werner, J. 'Mit Sehnsucht und Seelengepack in die Unendlichkeit'. *Publik-Forum Extra: Magazin für Spiritualität und Lebenskunst*, October 2007.

Wertsch, J. V. *Voices of Collective Remembering*. Cambridge, UK: Cambridge University Press, 2002.

Bibliography

Wijnandts, H. 'Ecological Energetics of the Long-Eared Owl (Asio Otus)'. *Ardea* 38–90 (2002): 1–92.

Williams, G. H. *Wilderness and Paradise in Christian Thought.* Menno Simons Lectures. New York: Harper & Brothers, 1962.

Williams, T. T. *Refuge: An Unnatural History of Family and Place.* 2nd ed. New York: Vintage Books, 2001.

Wood, D. 'Lynch Debord: About Two Psychogeographies'. *Cartographica: The International Journal for Geographic Information and Geovisualization* 45 (2010): 185–99.

Worman, C. O. 'Trooping fairies, trolls, and talking tigers: the influence of traditional wilderness archetypes on current land use patterns'. *Biodiversity and Conservation* 19 (2010): 3171–93.

Wyatt, N. 'The Vocabulary and Neurology of Orientation'. Pages 351–80 in *Ugarit, Religion and Culture.* Edited by N. Wyatt and W. G. E. Watson. Munster: Ugarit-Verlag, 1996.

Yair, A. 'The Ambiguous Impact of Climatic Change at the Desert Fringe'. Pages 199–227 in *Environment Change in Drylands.* Edited by A. C. Milington and K. Pye. New York: Wiley, 1994.

Yelena Helgasdóttir. 'Retrospective Methods in Dating Post-Medieval Rigmarole-Verses from the North Atlantic'. Pages 98–119 in *New Focus on Retrospective Methods: Resuming Methodological Discussions: Case Studies from Northern Europe.* Edited by E. Heide and K. Bek-Pedersen. Folklore Fellows' Communications 307. Helsinki: Suomalainen Tiedeakatemia, Academia Scientiarum Fennica, 2014.

Zahran, M. A., and A. J. Willis. *The Vegetation of Egypt.* London: Chapman & Hall, 1992.

Zarini, V. 'Aspects et paradoxes du désert dans une épopée latine de l'Afrique chrétienne du VIe siècle'. Pages 143–57 in *Le désert, un espace paradoxal.* Edited by G. Nauroy, P. Halen, and A.-E. Spica. Recherches en littérature et spiritualité 2. Bern: Lang, 2003.

Zimmermann, F. *The Jungle and the Aroma of Meats.* Comparative Studies of Health Systems and Medical Care 20. Berkeley: University of California Press, 1987.

INDEX

Aaron, 28
Abbey, Edward, 17, 48
Acacia, 14, 18
Adyton, 43–44
Alaska, 40
Amalekites, 47
Amos, 7
Anthony of the Desert, 38, 42, 44
Anzu Myth, 31
Apophatic Spirituality, 43
Aqaba, 3
Arabah, 6, 29
Arabia, 3, 23, 30, 60
Arapaho, 40
Archetypes, 4, 35–37, 41–42, 51, 72, 74
Arizona, 17, 40
Ashurnirari, 32
Aslan, 50
Assurbanipal, 31, 32
Athabaskan, 40
Athanasius, 42
Atonement, Day of, 31, 41
Australia, 48
Azazel, 31, 41

Baal, 32
Babylon, 31
Bahir, Book of, 41–42
Ballou, Hosea, II, 51
Balzac, Honoré de, 48
Bantu Peoples, 39–40
Basso, Keith, 29, 59, 63–64

Baudrillard, Jean, 12, 17, 29
Bedouin, 81
Beguines, 72
Boas, Franz, 64
Borella, Jean, 51, 59
Bourdieu, Pierre, 17
Broomtree, 14
Bryson, Bill, 14
Burckhardt, Titus, 74

Cardinal Directions, 40–41
Cassirer, Ernst, 51
Chronicles, Books of, 2, 28
Climate, 11, 18
Coetzee, Narelle J., 70
Cognitive Science, 11–12, 18, 26, 35, 52, 57
Cooper, James Fenimore, 81
Crumley, Carole, 3

Darom, 27–28
Debord, Guy, 19–20
Deleuze, Giles, 11
Demons, 31
Deuteronomy, 2, 6–8, 12, 28–29, 32, 42, 71–72
Dickens, Charles, 50
Directions, 26–28, 40
Djinn, 37

Eagles, 40
Eagle-owls, 12
Eckhart, Meister, 43–44, 72, 80
Ecopsychology, 59

Index

Edda, 38, 77
Edom, 2, 6–8, 14, 18, 20–21, 27, 29, 31, 42
Egypt, 12, 32, 37, 62
Eliade, Mircea, 35
Elijah, 28, 32, 42
Elisha, 32
Eloah, 7–8
Elves, 39, 77
Enneads, 43
Enunciative Linguistics, 30
Environmentalism, 47
Eriugena, John Scotus, 44, 80
Essenes, 42
Evans-Pritchard, E. E., 64
Exodus, 2, 28, 32, 41, 51
Ezekiel, 6, 7, 27–28, 32

Fairies, 75
Feldt, Laura, 31, 70
Folklore, 6, 13, 35–37, 40–42, 56–57, 75
Forests, 37–38, 57
Francis of Assisi, 42

Gazelle, 45
Geertz, Clifford, 4, 59, 64–65
Genesis, 7
Gerbils, 13
Ghosts, 18, 32
Gilgamesh, Epic of, 31
Goethe, Johann Wolfgang von, 20
Goethean Science, 19–20
Goodwyn, Erik, 35–36, 72
Grasshoppers, 13
Great Wilderness Debate, 47, 81
Gregory of Nyssa, 44
Greshake, Gisbert, 15, 60, 72, 83
Grimm, Jacob and Wilhelm, 77
Guattari, Félix, 11

Gunnell, Terry, 77

Habakkuk, 2, 7–8, 29, 50
Hadewijch of Brabant, 44
Hagar, 28
Havasupai People, 40
Hebron, 28
Heide, Eldar, 57
Heidegger, Martin, 11, 53
Heimskringla, 38
Hejaz, 3
Hinduism, 71
Hittites, 37
Holm, Ingunn, 60, 77
Homer, 37, 76
Homuncular, 26
Honko, Lauri, 56
Hoppal, Minhaly, 56
Hosea, 51
Ḥunafā', 48
Huxley, Aldous, 17, 20, 50
Hyenas, 12, 13
Hymes, Dell, 71
Hymns, 83

Iceland, 38
Inanna, 31
Infield and Outfield, 60
Insoll, Timothy, 18
Ireland, 37, 75
Isaiah, 2, 7, 12–13, 23, 28–29, 31, 42, 70
Ishmaelites, 47
Islam, 37, 42–43, 48, 60, 74

Jeremiah, 32, 41
Jeshimon, 29
Jesus, 48
Job, 7, 23, 27–28
Joel, 31
John van Ruysbroeck, 43, 44
Jonah, 23

Index

Jordan River, 3, 29
Joshua, 6–7
Judges, Book of, 6–8, 29
Jung, Carl, 35, 42, 51, 72, 74, 83
Jungian Psychology, 51, 74

Kabbalah, 41, 50
Kadesh Barnea, 6, 11, 21
Kafka, Franz, 11
Kalahari, 11
Kamba People, 40
Khamsin, 23
Kikuyu People, 40
Kings, Books of, 2, 6, 28, 32
Krutch, Joseph W., 17–18

Lakota, 47
Lane, Belden C., 50, 63
Lapis Lazuli, 37
Lawlor, David, 59
Lawrence, T.E., 23–24
Leach, Edmund, 35
Lettrists, 19
Lewis, C. S., 54
Lilith, 31
Lings, Martin, 74
Lugalbanda, 31
LugalE, 31
Lynch, Kevin A., 19

Magic, 64
Malinowski, Bronisław, 63–64, 71
McGinn, Bernard, 72, 79–80
Mechthild of Magdeburg, 43
Memorates, 56
Memory, 19
Menhirs, 7-
Merleau-Ponty, Maurice, 12
Mesopotamia, 23, 31
Metallurgy, 39

Metaphor, 2, 4, 36, 52, 56, 68, 75
Midbar, 28–29, 70
Midian, 2, 14, 18, 21, 27, 42
Moab, 17
Monotheism, 41, 45, 48
Monsters, 40
Moses, 28, 42, 44
Moslund, Sten, 11
Motifs, 8, 26, 35–36, 72
Mountains, 2, 6, 28–29, 31, 37, 40–41, 47, 76, 81, 83
Muhammed, 48
Mysticism, 18, 42–44, 72

Navajo, 40, 78
Negev, 3, 13–15, 18, 20, 23, 26, 28, 30
Neo-Platonism, 43–44
Nilotic Peoples, 39
Nomads, 3, 12
Numbers, Book of, 28, 42–43
Numinous, 41, 68

Odyssey, 37
Orientalism, 47
Owls, 12, 13, 28

Panchatantra, 38
Paran, 2, 6–7, 13, 29, 31, 51, 84
Participant Observation, 16–18, 20, 47, 63–66
Phenomenology, 17
Philo of Alexandria, 42
Plotinus, 43
Polytheism, 48
Porcupines, 12
Pragmatics, 30
Procksch, Otto, 70
Psalms, 7–8, 28–29, 56, 70
Pseudo-Dionysius the Areopagite, 44, 80

Index

Psychogeography, 19, 67

Qur'an, 37, 48

Recurrent Multiword Sequences, 6, 8, 72
Rhineland Mystics, 43, 44

Samuel, Books of, 2, 28
Sand, 13–14, 23–24, 38, 81
Sapir, Edward, 71
Saussure, Ferdinand de, 30
Seir, 2, 6–8, 29, 31
Serpents, 31
Shamanism, 38
Shamash, 75
Shoshone People, 40
Silence, 17, 20–21, 50
Sinai, 2–3, 6–8, 14, 29, 51
Sinuhe, Tale of, 37
Sirocco, 23
Situationism, 19
Snorri Sturluson, 38, 77
Sociolinguistics, 71
Sperber, Dan, 35
Spirituality, 83
Storms, 2, 8, 23, 40
Surrealism, 20
Suso, Henry, 43
Szlamowicz, Jean, 4, 51

Tabari, Al-, 48
Talmon, Shemaryahu, 72
Tarazi, Paul Nadim, 70
Tauler, Johannes, 43
Teman, 2, 7–8, 26–28, 43, 51, 83

Theophany, 2, 9, 33
Tilley, Christopher, 17, 26
Tolkien, J. R. R., 26
Toponyms, 29
Topopoetics, 11
Tortoises, 13
Trees, 18, 23
Trolls, 38, 77
Tsiyya, 29

Ugarit, 26, 31
Umar ibn al–Khaṭṭāb, 15
Utah, 17

Wadis, 14
Whirlwinds, 23–24
Wilderness Wanderings, 32
Wind, 21, 23–4, 27–28, 40–41, 50
Witchcraft, 64
Witches, 50, 64, 77
Wolves, 12, 29, 60
Wood, Denis, 17
Worman, Cedric O'Driscoll, 36
Wormwood, 14
Wyatt, Nicolas, 26–27

Yahweh, 5, 8
Yahwism, 2–3
Yamin, 26

Zande People, 64
Zechariah, 2, 8, 23, 29
Zohar, 41